Édouard Glissant

Poetic Intention

*translated from the French by*
Nathanaël
with Anne Malena

Nightboat Books
Callicoon, NY

Cover and Interior Design: typeslowly

Cataloging-in-publication data is available from the Library of Congress

Nightboat Books
Callicoon, New York
www.nightboat.org

# Table of Contents

# Histories

The fugitive – the African bound for the deleterious islands – did not even recognize the taste of night. This unknown night was less dense, more naked, alarming. Far behind him he heard the dogs, but already the acacias had abducted him from the world of hunters; in this way he entered, man of the grande terre, into another history: where, unbeknownst to him, the times were beginning again for him. He would never have the leisure of shouting: "oh in July 1788 I fled to the heights" – but, as though crammed into the minuscule enclosure of earth, in the violent squall of mornes circled by seas, he would spell: "nor had I emerged from the death of the boat than I was already a runaway on the trail of the acacias": then he would lead his children to that place where, after having set beneath the stump tangled head and beast (silt and vines), he had slept his first night.

These dogs, too, had crossed the sea. Mastiffs of Flanders or of the Black Forest. But they were not entering into this other history: masters and dogs had come for plunder and profit, soon they would want to extend their land into these parts. The new history did not disturb them, though they were about to make it. Only this one here was split, who lived in hiding on the Trace and knew the Acoma.

Today the cane shoots push their rusty nudities toward the dark green of the heights. What was retreat, trembling, the furor of being and the smoke of charcoal gave way little by little to fertilizer. The histories, the split, became reduced, unified. The times are given one to the other. Yet who returns to the incline of the mornes, and rummages? There, before the hut, is an old man who knows nothing of "poetry", and whose voice alone is *opposed*. Gray hair on his black head, he carries in the melee of lands, in the two histories, the pure and stubborn power of a root. He persists, he treads the fallow land that does not procure. (For him the depths, the possibilities of voice!) I saw his eyes, I saw his stray eyes seek the space of the world.

"SUN OF CONSCIOUSNESS"

The One, the flourish of stars which perhaps comprise the unattackable body of Truth. Yes, every passion of the world, of the living, of the tremor by which being is provoked, begins with this consensual lack: the One. And each persuades himself that the One is abrupt, that it is only attainable through outburst, through spark and revelation. Generous naiveté, but a necessary ardor, without which departure is defective, hardened. To move beyond the ecstatic ambition of the One is to build with patience, without denying the primordial burst, the stages of a knowledge at long last approached. The œuvre in its continuity traces this itinerary, beyond which, perhaps, the more or less victorious accidents which are its markers or, to the letter, its milestones: books.

But how does one distract the œuvre from the works which comprise it? Might there be an "intention" (which one?) which would go along this journey, inseparable from the more or less imperfect matter that books would propose? And, consequently, that from a series of unfinished works a livable lesson might emerge? Or, more improbable yet, that in an accumulation of perfectly organized matter might the unconvincing stagnate and putrefy?

If an "intention" of an œuvre is at liberty to be legitimized, at the same time the book would have to be examined by its light and its shadow: when it frees this intention and when it smothers it.

And from then on, it would be possible to "hatch" what the intention, which governs the book and that the book accomplishes, has preserved or lost by realizing itself there. And if it is in effect possible to examine the distance between intention and the œuvre, then we are justified in freeing the notion of a "willful" literature (in which intention gains over the unpredicted part which hitherto belonged to the hazardous realm of the book). It is this possibility which first solicits me here, before falling again, definitely, obsolete: intention, even "willful", will die realizing itself.

We run the risk, some of us, of such an extracted literature. What matters, for this moment, to those who are born to the world, in a desperate world whose only common measure is excess, disparateness and opposition. But this birth is arduous: we grow faster than our words can say.


Since that time when I evoked, not walking in the streets (no gate was described, no passerby cited), but the patient absence of one who, while wandering, found in himself the inane force to hope – (far from any act which might have supported him, far from any sun, and even farther from a country where he buried himself in his soil at last) – since that time the We, postulated more than real, came more broadly to light. And so many hypotheses devoted to the growth of being did in fact materialize. The horizon of dreams, desires, obscure impulses toward that livable center, here is what stood out: some plain became larger and some city named. The world suddenly found itself large with those countries that still yesterday thickened in the night. The cry of their inhabitants was heard. The blood of earth ran into the earth.

It is not legitimate for me to consign here the cost then to others, the cost today of this clearing of the world. The suffering of peoples is not speakable; only their hope, their presence. Accompanying the horizon, as gradually on its ridges the curve of new cities became visible, there surfaced fighting men. Half the world came out of the nights, the half that had until then been marked to be the dark face of the globe. And here the earth became one, and in this density the One, mandated by the imaginary, was confirmed. The poetic ecstasy of the One is untied by militant unity.

But the One is harmonic; it is full of itself, and like a god it is enough to nourish its dreams. The unity of the world is, on the contrary, burdensome, its thickness in contrast to the drive of the Vow. The earth only combines forces with itself in order to judge the other: it is a struggle whose melee is everywhere. As much as the One appeared to be inaccessible, unity is arduous to conquer. Let us leave the dreams of childhood, the daydream of Truth; deny the One. Yet we will not be granted the clear harmony of the world. Because what is lacking eternally from the One is this realized dream – the Œuvre – that we would want to offer, from our awakenings; but what the unity of the world needs is that part of the world which, shivering in its being, is saddled with non-existence. Our only true cartage will distract nothing from the richness of the banks. On the banks, see so many savors that you ignore, you who are on the waves. There will be no depth for you, if you underestimate the shore. The One, the unique-in-the-world-and-in-being, needs what is missing also from the concrete unity of the earth: the wind coming off the shores, where so many of Us churn a little known silt. Every tribe that is lost, decried, separates us from harmony.

How is it possible to conclude starting at a landscape? Does "the banyan rain tree" shade a message other than that of willows? Are there no men who carry unruly jungles inside, where others secrete meadows? Do these not produce, every time, except in these contrary dictions, good breeding, a "style"?

When I believe this, all of a sudden the barely falling snow appears ineluctable. All it takes is the slightest layer, for the rain and the cars to disperse in a moment, for the immemorial fall to impose itself on me. Others shout: "Such slush!" and me, I see the uniformly white plain such as it had perhaps been last December. This snow compels me, even as it hesitates to establish itself. Something in me offers itself to the cold and the solitude, which can stand neither one nor the other: this cold cannot be evaluated by the degree of temperature, nor this solitude by the absence of people.

We create our landscapes, we decorate them with our fourail, with the blood that we dream of losing on the plant, and we brush against the delible scar. Then: when our landscape combines cleanly with the lines of a country we suddenly discover to be *ours*, then (the vow fulfilled, the impatience dried up, the silence and leisure of the work ideal offered up), the dream of the One, formerly abandoned, gathers us once more into its tyranny. So that we will leave it soon. Because intention and its progression have become rooted: of what I write, what remains to be written escapes despite myself.

How to conclude. When the sidereal paths of space will open to man, what will he recognize of earth, he who will return from *distant countries*? Not that series of landscapes that we discover there (in us), but a single signifying expanse, where the banyan tree will shade the meadow. This is what each hopes to see: the earth emerging from the abyss and thickening before oneself. Whoever finds the earth thus suspended in space, and who will come near, will nonetheless not experience the ecstasy of the One. For other stars will join themselves as pendants to this unique ball, which will already obsess the traveler. We must exhaust our landscapes, in other words, realize them. But we must not fear discovering them endlessly: new, tempting, possibly prohibited.

Contrary to what is usually avowed, I concede that I have always had in mind the project of this work. (You clear – you root – that same trunk. You write the same word.) So much (needless) repetition, so much "obviousness", for so long and these multiple strata of writing, each thought cleared from the soil, each swath tumbled from the poem converged toward that gathering. Lands accumulated little by little, where a furrow blinks incessantly augured by those distant times. *Sun of Consciousness*: *errance* introduced to diversity, then diversity forces being toward its "sense".

And, weaving an arbitrary or ambitious tie of the future œuvre to the world always present, I continue, by opening onto the perspective of the world the two shutters closed against the œuvre: the pile of matter, then its "significance". Immediately this new question, unformulated raving, sinews and glimmers there: what we call *depth* – the always fallow aspect of man – and what we call *totality* – the considerable widening of the horizon – are they as distantly complementary as we believe them to be? Today, would a signifying poetics, which would surprise the "total" matter of the world, conflict with a poetics of "depth"?

Matter, significance, depth and totality elect one another. The significance of matter, yes, that is its reality: not only its innervated, structured depth, but its considered breadth as well. Depth: significance that may well be hidden, but also law of relation between all matter. Now there is no depth to explore (no structure to track, no way to clear, no encryptable communication) apart from totality. What, of totality, again, and by return, if not the relation of each matter to *all* others.

Also you cannot disregard any one fact of the world. That is why the mute man who nonetheless speaks to you, speaks for you. For you also. For we must exhaust our landscapes, where we starkly illuminate structures (by "retreating" them). Maybe it is in fact the universal flourish of stars which comprise the One. (Hence: the sovereign landscape, radiant totality.) But perhaps also their action in man's solitude, lone witness. (And their design, lone force.) That is why, when we discover these aspects, we must attach ourselves to clearing them, not only in depth, but also in totality.


The work of this man is imperfect. You can huddle him in his shadow. Exegetes, barely will you concede that he has somewhat thickened the surrounding atmosphere. But you, travelers also, who consider the world without mixing with it, think that your work, which is carried before the world, is, if it so happens, already outmoded. You do not embrace the relation (denied or victorious) of totality to itself. You do not cease to want to be the *constitutive gaze* of the world. It is like a barrier that you set up between the body of the world and yourself. (And in saying so, I bring myself "before" my reality, in imbalance, alone confronted by this diction, where I should have enacted my birth to the world. But to say so is to attempt an other relation, a new relay: it is to be *touched* by you, and perhaps to consent. We do not escape the other). Your abstraction deviates, it seriates from an absence. Your work is perfect: it obliterates, once more.

From the series of imperfect works carried out by this man hitherto mute emerges a lesson. It is his labor (birthing himself) which completes and opens *the relational embodied in the world*. Every fertile abstraction nourishes itself of its fruitful imperfection. But your often abstract thought in relation to what it proposes to you (of the image of you that you find suddenly within it) and not in relation to what it is, even less what it is becoming (or will be). In other words these elucidations on which you meditate from his labor, suffer from not having been lived, from being inactual (not becoming). You surmise (or propose) a relation of what you are, were or will be to what this mute man appears to you to be, but not to what he is, was or will be. You define yourself in your relativities but you conceive him as *absolute*: who must not change and who cannot intrude on your territory. Your poetics is not tainted by his becoming which, if different, nonetheless regulates, and inversely, your own.

The œuvre. Taking the path again, knotting backwards the bond between the world and it, we distract it from books. Imperfect, unaccomplished in this man hitherto mute, it is important to the concept. And the concept orients us, even when it leans against the vision, not in the thick experience of the world. But how can we see the world without living it: it is seemingly what you have achieved with your immunity. Maybe it is necessary to distance oneself (cross once more the sea, eternal obstacle to knowledge), in order to feel that it is stupid and unjust that you seem to hold the exclusivity of the concept, and that the mute man is considered the privileged receptacle of the passion of the world. That is one category whose formulation is rendered ephemeral by the opening of the world. There are no outdated thoughts which perish beside new energies that are uncontrolled, naïve, rudimentary. Thanks in part to you, history introduced these separations. History must be assumed *completely* (lived together) in order perhaps to move beyond it (like the sea) once more.

They call it Finistère: the end (or the tip) of lands. And that was its extremity. We approached it along stone ravines, as if drawn by this tranquil desolation, impatient (or anxious) to reach that point beyond which, in all appearances, there is nothing. Every country, for he who inhabits it, spurs on a finistère. But over there, there is something else. You learn, solitaries of all times who have marked out the world, that there is something over there. The sea spells it for you. From the edge of your earth, here is the sea that opens and that unites. You were its servants, indeed you also subdued it; there remains of it a taste of solitude, of regret, in your body. Here is the sea, and here is the other. The unnoticed difference, too strongly felt. The interval, unaccepted, endured too much. The wave of the world against your Mounts. I saw them shiver with a present over there which opened another space to them, where they were not used to balancing. The pewter of the horizon moved the gray stained voice of the unified toward them. Clouds covered the voice, as if to protect those who, between two labors, came there to scrutinize the shade from elsewhere. Strolling, at the end of their universe, of their week. Dressed in their Sunday's best, vacant, serene. Their lives fell drunk into the sea.

To be born into the world. But *was not this* world, yesterday, in those and for those who were now "being born"? Each elects his world as a universe when the universe is unknown or misunderstood. For a long time the world was thus an idea of the world, world-as-solitude, or -as-identity, enlarged from the sole evidence of the known particular and enclosing the All as a pure extension of that particular. He who went far from home, the Discoverer, and he who remained on his land, the to-discover, shared that common belief. To be born into the world, is at last to conceive (to live) the world as a relation: as a composed necessity, a consenting reaction, a poetics (and not morality) of alterity. As the incomplete drama of that necessity.

Into this we are born; and you, discoverers. For from the world-as-solitude to the world-as-relation, you have only travelled the part of the path on which, discovering the world, you determined that it was a world-as-imposition, as a univocal tragedy, then as a world-as-totality but without the relation: yes, as a totalitarian world. All particular forms of the totalitarian, in and out of your walls, come from that concept of the world and garner their authority from it. Solitude in the world (identity projected from the world and from oneself) was developed by you into one solitude among others (as an identity imposed by the world and by oneself).

To be born into the world will consist for you in rending consent from yourselves, and for the other in rending the distance – the right to distance: the consciousness of the self liberated in the relation is the to-be-built of the other, and on the contrary the relation liberated in-side the consciousness of the self, your work. You say: *overseas* (we said it with you), but you too will soon be overseas.

To be born to the world is for each to enter abrupt and knowledgeable into the simple or thrashed truth of one's materiality, knowing that that which is not destined to a relation to the other is worthless. In the now multivocal and every day provoked tragedy (where the bloody assault of the Same also shatters to death the peoples) is outlined and carried through the common vocation of the tragedists that we are.


There is a universal as vow, in which the being without orient is caught. *The eternal fixation of days and sobs.* Moreover, what relay? No end is possible here: from every infertile unscrambled chaos proceeds a *deep* chaos which is to be wholly cleared. The aspiration (the pretention) to the universal must be interred in the dark secret soil where each lives his relation to the other. The poetics of this shared quotidian is fastened in the succulence of *your* country. (As long as you display the succulence to the aspects of the other, as long as you elect it before the other and tie them together.) If in the sands of your shore you unearth the rusted sword of the other, clean it and make yourself a hoe from it. If the sword becomes inflamed in the hands of the other, grab it, or try to grab it, to arm the other – as much as yourself – with the same vow. Such is the vow.

The sole end being actual here, limited, threatened: that the universal as absolute carries in its very avatars the possible, which becomes the relation as truth, and manœuvers it despite itself. Ensuring this state, confirming this condition. Relation is not lived absolutely (it would deny itself), it is felt in reality. If one day it spreads in satiation, man will have secreted other shores, other hoes. Here and now, the poetics seriates and marries the savors of countries, at the same time as it casts them into the felt knowledge not of the Other but of the relation to the known other.

When the poet travels to the ends where there is no country, he opens with the more deserved relation, in that space of an *absolute elsewhere* in which each can attempt to reach him. (Artaud, Michaux; who so completely razed the outworn psychologies into which were crammed the poetics of the Occident; men whom one could only approach in the beyond of relations, where every relation has already been accomplished; predecessors and unencircled, who have *in themselves* cleared from their own ground the factitious traces, fallowed the honourable fields; backwards labourers, *in reverse*). The relation does not consent to the footpaths of tradition, but surfaces impure from all chaos lived there and by all illuminated.

To be born into the world is to be aware, to suffer, to feel the energy of this share, heavy to carry, stern to say.


The visitor compliments: "Here is the country of perpetual summer!" But perpetual summer couldn't be summer. For within summer stalks or sleeps the first winter which – besides autumn – will accomplish summer. Here there is the Unique Season. A force from which at each moment and in the moment we forge ourselves. I saw, I can say so: uncovered, this morning a tiny and black crested bird, whose name I don't know and who has no age. I was suddenly attentive to nature. In this bird, the only fire. He trembled an instant beneath a branch, and was gone toward the sea, down there. I have no concern for where he comes from, and don't seek to know where he is going. Only the instant of his presence. After, I am no longer attentive to Nature. The Unique Season of this bird is the same: it forces us without fail to know it, but doesn't oblige us to meditate on it. No alternation here rotates the crops of thought. Yet a continuous gravity fixes it. For us to establish that this fixation is of the root and not of debris. For us to seek, in the Unique Season, the measure of time, and imagine where it comes from with us and to know toward what it accompanies us.

The End is relay. It is not the being of the Other that is imposed on me but the modality of my relation to him: and inversely.

So it happens that a perfect arrangement of materials makes the unconvincing stagnate and wallow. For the poetics of relation assumes that to each is proposed the density (the opacity) of the other. The more the other resists in his thickness or his fluidity (without being limited to it), the more his reality becomes expressive, and the more fecund the relation. The un-obvious is that which by its mass or its stretched aptness illuminates. Schéhadé proves it: innocently? Opacity will hold us back yet, which fascinates and precipitates. Similarly, in the historical preparation, the troubled being has the burden of proof, in the place where the being braced against his being closes the night of isolation (which is not illuminating opacity) over himself. Relation is not a mathematics of rapport but a problematic that is always victorious over threats. To live the relation may very well be to measure its convincing fragility.

To track angelism here. It is vanity, immediately drowned in the din of bombs and the echo of tortures, to pose the relation as a substitute for the absolute (of ideal perfection: in which man is a lamb before man); it requires that in lived experience, multiplied for oneself and for the other, the mass of the quotidian be encirclable in its detail: the relation is not prophetic, it plays every day of the world. Every technique of apprehension, every system of expression, every meticulousness, every machinery, are of concern to it. Its poetics does not in any way dispense itself from investing in them. The most humble improvement of the slightest detail of life is of interest to the relation. The latter intertwines world politics (the adjusting efforts of peoples who confront and are attuned to one another) and its ill-being (the privation of men before the unsuspected field of satiation). The resulting expression is grave and communicable.

Three times the œuvre is of concern. In that it is the urge of a group of men: community; in that it is tied to the vow of a man: intention; in that it is human labor and tragedy that continue here: relation. The ground of the group, the language of that man, the duration for the human: thus, the elements of the poetics, ventured from one to the other. For every group in its justice takes on the time of men, and every man gives himself over to the earth on which he knows felicity, and every humanity builds its language from languages: and so on through infinite references. Yet now the group suddenly imposes its word, humanity devastates its own lands, man loses in time the time of his history. Today the world of relation is very much a fertilizable tragedy, mortal melee, Promethean chaos. Neither the *constitutive gaze* nor analysis are enough to disentangle them: if you are not drama and melee in this chaos, you will dry out in your removed clarity. That is, you yourself will keep to your drama (stranger in your strangeness), where, if it happens, already the obviousnesses of shared tragedy, never closed, always fecund, will wait for you, watch for you, deceive you. So what does it matter whether the content be mystical or metaphysical, bequeathed yesterday by the vow of the poet or the powerlessness of the pronouncer to the Other. And what do the hidden objective motivations matter of those who advanced along the hard path of the Other: it is enough for us here that they hailed the Other and followed the path. Poets have reasons despite their unsignified reasons.

(Like a people, peopled with hecatombs, whom we seduce
With the greedy duration of its tomb, like a wind that
    destroys itself –
What do they say of poetry, to hold tight or scrutinize, when
    the noise
Of the tide elects itself, and when we must quiet that noise?
    Summer
Was thought, pearly idea, the pure product of your impurity.
Upon you summer is unhauled, the summer anchor has
    landed us
Me the ship you the pier! Me thickness and you duration.
    Here,
I told them the obscure hideout of our hoard. I told them
Rock not slag, oh! collected water that isn't rain!
And it is reserve of science as well as an abyssal wine in his
    childhood.

We must leave this edge and move toward the fertilizers
Night in our loins has not yet grown its fire
And we haven't pierced the black idea of our noise on the tide.


Your beach burns. Gutted by its rocks. A raw
Jolt. Water that wavers enchants and falls, and drunken, too
Deaf, to wander! On your cliffs kept so pure by the fire
To Fall – It's you that I seek, I seek you and I create you
Pure to lure me, tide! Believing I've seized your noise,
Like a people dried up in your country or one drowned, drowned
In the thickness of purity! When opacity runs from me
I venerate you on your land which only gapes at its midnight.
   Here,
To the idea among this day to sacrifice your nudity
I raise myself on the tide – but I seek you, you create me
Country aggrieved with sores. What are they saying to haul
   you to shout you?
Among the swallowing of acacias and hedges? – You are afraid
   of loving.
Your purity is there impure and more thick, where I drowned.)

(To consign the "planetarization" of thought is therefore making the avowal of man in a novel situation: grappling with himself – with his "totality" – for the first time: conscious or troubled in all respects of himself that he – Occidental – had managed until then to misjudge, even overlook, or – non-occidental – mistake, even withstand. After having learned with psychoanalysis that he is responsible for a fallow "aspect", the man of the Occident experiences those "parts" of humanity he had not been aware of, that (despite Montaigne's cautions) he hadn't need to "consider": those that populated the chasms. *The maimed.* He discovers and experiences them, where until now he had only contemplated them. He has been the irresistible vehicle of the world. But he dismembered himself between the function that was his own and that he had conquered (being the relayer of the world) and the ambition he held (to be the world's absolute). The "universal" he promoted turned out to be so abstract, so ideal in the conception that was made of it and the expression it was granted, – that it became possible to combine it with any other particular value, as long as it had the audacity to prohibit throwing it into question. So the man of the Occident believed himself to be "living the life of the world", where often he only reduced the world and suffused it with an ideational globality – which was not at all totality of the world.

The poets suffered and generously expressed this distance that ideologies or systems tended to deny or mask.

Contesting the predominance of the Occident, at the same time the other of the world *integrated* it into the world. Underscoring the "active" in the operation. The Occident, which had dominated the world, hadn't, beyond palpable gain and the mind's advantage, been *interested* in it; contesting the Occident, the rest of the world takes the active relay and constitutes the powerful factor in one of the elements, not a predominant one, of a possible planetary civilization. In this way he accepts and integrates it. He *forces* it into relativity. Each of the current "zones" of humanity is preoccupied with its neighbor (they are all neighbors) but also occupies it. We are all, and at the same time, the fallow aspect, the unconscious, the unknown (excessively known) part of the other. – Was not what you would call History incomplete, not only in reach but yet in "understanding"? Is there not in your weary disdain for the historical a sort of affront to those who never had a history for you? The history you ignored – or didn't make – was it not History? (The complex and mortal *anhistorical*). Might you not be more and more affected by it, in your fallowness as much as in your harvest? In your thought as much as in your will? Just as I was *affected* by the history I wasn't making, and could not ignore?

This concrete presence of *diversified* peoples, this function they fill on the new horizon, it seems to me that we feel them everywhere, we sometimes become irritated with them, but we tend toward consecrating them. The most lucid individuals fear the breath of the world. The extermination of a people by another is a product of that *panic* as much as of politics: the terror of having to abdicate the exclusivity of one's wealth is bound to the repulsion of *sharing the being-of-the-world*. Which is, at another level, that of the most absolute nobility and responsibility (in which a being suffers from what he says), the systematic intellectual attitude of derision is fleshed out in the unconscious refusal of sharing of oneself, of living the world and the thought of the world with the other. The unhappy consciousness appears then as complete generosity – presuming every surge is unmotivated – with naiveté. Rammed in those famous garbage bins, the last and theatrical refuge of desperate lucidity, the trunk-man, having himself amputated his own legs, forces himself in this way to refuse to *walk*. Just like that – conscience-nescience is yet more knowledgeable and alive than the classical satisfaction in which the western self – whether in refusal or imposition – is often adorned.

That is perhaps one of the more serious avatars of "planetary thought", which could only have been sensed or first marked out in the Occident – Kostas Axélos for example published a series of studies which all carry (it's the title of the book) *Toward planetary thought* – in other words where the opportunity of knowledge already enables *thinking*, but could not have appeared or been developed into a problematic (sensed or "formulated") without the contestatory effort of those who (we have said as much: rending law from distance) are born to the world. Yet this birth to the world modifies the world and the man who lives it. The *will to participate*, at a time when every act is motivated by reason or by wrong, could not be abdicated in the reassuring deduction according to which, in any way, each lives the life of the whole earth. The technical benefit and methodological advantage could render beings bound to the *game of the world*. To accept (deep within oneself) this relativized world, to overcome the selfish fear of sinking into it, to transmute reflective solitude into shared inflection – is that not the more exact way of truly accomplishing one's own methods, one's vocation, one's poetics?)

# POETIC INTENTION

(Such a startling condition, that a man withstands being so hunted by an artifice, that simply to say what he is requires him to proclaim what he isn't, and that before naming himself he has to incite the names that fasten him from such a distance. And not only him. Not that face with its innumerable solitude, but solitude, silence

Their enormity, without drains or hills nor a ravine for crouching while awaiting the pounce. Where so many withhold calling out the name, and so many, hiding in themselves for falling short of the path, decline to exist without naming themselves. Believing that to call one's name in one's land when it is naked will unleash calamity.

They count on their self to intimate them,

Their heart more frozen than the kidney of a mongoose touched at the loin, breathless, who turns to death *in* itself to spit at the spearhead serpent's venom.


I say what I am not, in a common way and to admit everything about these futile  days: one requires of me a guarantee that this is no sectarian remark, the other that I prove it – or: "It's useless,

What business does it have in the universal fields of poetry?"

And the pack of parched selves rushes at those morsels of meat.

Poetry in its intention maintains that the being cover his earth without being charged by the forces of order to prove; that he become alarmed and reject without being decried by doctrine for alacrity; that he travel the world along the arduous footpath between all languages; — but that he also weigh the non-departed vertigo of his density,

Thus on his soil the acoma, which breathes with Fomalhaut.)

There is no intention that resists the upsurge from the imagined. But there is no œuvre that, while developing, doesn't arm itself with a single constant and often incommunicable intention. This one, yet to be accomplished, immediately masks itself; this centre, illuminated, becomes stellated. At the same time the project, for being diffuse and soon disseminated, gathers, fortifies itself. Double volley: what is imagined deports the subject, little by little the subject fixes the imaginary and the sum.

So for the writer, what he writes is bit by bit but the draft of what henceforth (there, ceaselessly) he will write. Better, what he will write will be but the shadow of what he should write (of what in eternity he would be destined to write, if eternity were his). For writing, like the same, is a consensual lack. The œuvre that does not suffer this absence is thereby a testament to narrow-mindedness; works of pleasure are complete. This is more striking when the author has had the time (denied to Balzac) to carry the œuvre to its projected "end": À la recherche du temps perdu leads that distant and sought after truth, encircled and fugitive, captive and elsewhere triumphant. And Faulkner's project, so many times taken up again, escapes the cadence of his books. As the being approaches the realization of intention, he discovers that the created reality is not, properly speaking, the one he had ambitioned, and that the truth of the intention was ripening less in his intentional consciousness than in the subconscious mass of facts understood by intention. The œuvre that achieves its purpose reveals another (hidden) purpose of the author's, and which remains open: to be accomplished. The writer is always the ghost of the writer he wants to be.

Obviousness? That is only worth examining if we carry it to its extreme consequences. It would seem in effect that certain œuvres are self-*sufficient*, because they assume in their principle that the realized intention will open onto a given that will not be an (other) hidden purpose of the author, but the manifested experience of a people. These œuvres break the circle: "author's explicit intention – reality of the work – author's unrealized hidden intention" and *distribute* it thus: "author's (explicit or non-explicit) intention – reality of the work – (manifested) intention of a people". It could be the *Aeneid*, at any rate the *Divine Comedy*, certainly the *Iliad* and the *Odyssey*. There, any future of the work is given in the work. And all the more when the work, including a humanity uncertain of its riches, does not impose a meaning on wealth. The *Aeneid* is indeed more "willful" than the *Iliad* and *The Divine Comedy* certainly totalizes man's history and universe, as far even as the regions of God. Yet to seek and to impose a meaning to wealth was adventurous, where once gathering and seriating that wealth (with scholarly innocence?) was: the *Aeneid* is far, in echoes, from the *Iliad*. But Virgil works his will over already fixed matter, the Roman Empire; compared to him, Dante is deep with totalizing matter in the making (Italy in its aggregation and its expression, the unanimous and metaphysical Occident at the moment of its vocation). But Dante suffers, vis-à-vis the Homeric works, from his will to universalize, to totalize, to systematize: he whom we call Homer is a receptor as though collective, who *gathers*.

Hegel analyzed these categories of the Epos at length. We see that the *total* book (in which the expressed matter does not seem to suffer from the *absence* that I mentioned) is on all counts a *common* book (common to a people: binding that people in its first unanimity). Next, that the ancient weakness of the "common" *willful* œuvre (in relation to the one it instinctively synthesized) could, in this time of split consciousness, carry itself with force and some advantage. Finally, that this advantage would be to extend from the œuvre to the literature that it inaugurates and nonetheless gives rise to it.

Exasperating ignorance, which confines to occidental designs. Hunched into that history, I aspire to experience as many births as were lived by the peoples. I am happy with the miserable overview. Such a bracketing of man's history (Histories). Really each history (and as a result each Reason for History projected on it) has decidedly been the exclusion of the others: this is what consoles me for having been excluded by Hegel from the historical movement. "What we understand in sum under the name Africa is an undeveloped anhistorical world, a prisoner entirely of the natural spirit and whose place is still found at the threshold of universal history." In which totalizing Reason was less poetic, insightful, than Montaigne's tolerant relativism. The Hegelian investigation of the world, so beautifully systematic and so profitable to occidental methodologies, stumbles against details where Montaigne's interest dryly exerts itself. Thus Hegel is himself a prisoner at times of the parenthesis in which (despite that *still* of the last clause) he encloses the African.

For if I now examine the Occident, I see that it has decidedly not stopped conceiving of the world first as solitude and then as imposition – of the Occident. (Such that the conceptual relegation of Africa far from "universal history" will be accompanied and followed by a real bracketing of African history; the lack of observed development will be systematized into profitable under-development; and the Black man, considered by Hegel as a being of innocence, will be turned by Gobineau into a being of impulse and by the colonizer a being of indolence: the most grandiose views of Reason, imperative and non relational, degrade imperceptibly into that solitude I described.)

Now I can only sketch out this truth: I group myself together with the I that is the we of a people; because I was born with it to the evidence of its history, of its country, of its soon to be consensual relationship to the other. And though I may live truncated or denatured, it will still be in what follows from a history of that we: I might be an avatar of the we, who says I with me "here".

And if I want then to understand my state in the world, I see that it is not for the malicious pleasure of contradicting Hegel after the fact, nor to take naive revenge on him, that I tend to rummage through my history: immediately I must catch those enormous expanses of silence in which my history became lost. Time, duration, are for me imperious vitalities. But I have also to live and proclaim actuality *with* the others who are living it. On good grounds. That which is then a poetics, in the larger poetics of relation, is thus contradictorily bound in urgency: the cry lived in the assumed duration, the duration lived in the reasoned cry.

Here the rocks seem of earth; amalgamated with chalk blood they sponge themselves and root in the red tuff.

Their lair is congested with lost corpses, ghost bodies (who, for having been sewed into the depths of time, forgotten there, grew their vehement rot into the rock)

of those whom at the first we called our heroes, and whom we sing in truth,

they who are not aflame in the unique light of verified posterity

but who keep watch in the deafness of this rock, awaiting our cry to convoke them.


We cry out, but the cry dwindles that can open neither rocks nor earth.

Men kill themselves with cutlass blows; their yellowed eyes are blind, their hand pitiful.

Those who own own nothing, derision sings its quadrille for them.

Women pass through their bodies, and the force in them lies unemployed.

The visitor, surprised by the ruins, looks distractedly at the rock.

He doesn't know that anonymous bodies watch there, who await our true cry to undo themselves.


And if I try to sound this marvel of civilizations that the Occident collects, I marvel that so much grandeur rested on such narrow imposition: that only in the dignity of the human person (that can only here be rallied to the frantic defence of private property) did this destiny draw its source. That no anonymous (collective) hero – besides the unknown soldier: not anonymous but elected and hidden (symbolic) – has been celebrated. That of Phaedra and Œdipus and Hamlet, the individual – even and especially because responsible for the common upsurge – first exalted its secret liberty. That no community here be stripped of its individualities: so much that the physical or ontological salvation of communities required that the individual be immolated, whose "prophetic" death guaranteed the life and salvation of the City. That on these two injunctions – the one summary and how rigid: property; the other arduous and always yet to conquer: interior liberty – the conquest of being and world was played. That the most absolute communities were only extracted *against* this drive. And here indeed the enormous system of truths, of powers, of worries and depths (without surveying their methods and techniques) were conquered.

But I am saying that this history is not mine, and that for me there is a depth and a complexity of *common consent* which, in the unrest of the being, comes each time to reverse the order of dignity and elect it as a mutely shared vocation. (So many "socialisms", it's true, drive their "just-about" out of this observation.) That there is nothing more obvious, nor more fecund, but something like another indice of being. That these dead scorched in the forgotten earth call our voices. Without our having in turn to shout, as before the umpteen wave of enemies: "Rise up, dead!")

Yet what would we do in the world, one and other (and those of whom I have yet no knowledge), who carry so many contrary motivations? Outside of the time when technologies and fixed weapons will have procured domination for you, advantage, leisure of reflection, — what will we do? How will we fashion our contrary quakes, — other than by the relation that is not simply impact nor contact, but further on the implication of spared and integrated opacities?

The poetics of duration endeavours to appease the feverish yesterday, to weave that distant becoming.

And I do not contend that pure, innocent communities were the prerogative of those whom today I call my ancestors, and from whom I am only descended after detour and voyage (murky condition of being). I want to resist praising at every turn what is obscure and little known to me. But what is patent is that never on the lands of these ancestors did myth so tenaciously cultivate this unique and shadowy fruit: the individual closed over his abyssal liberty; that never did the bloody effort of societies attempt to perpetuate so ferociously the very root of the fruit: private property.

I can also see that in my country and on my land *the title* belongs to others; that the land is not in us; murky condition once again, that rails at and rallies the poetics of being. That this land where so many anonymous ones sealed by the history of others (by denial and oblivion) no longer sleep, that this land thus fertilized with the blood of a people, not only does not belong to that people (in it, and yet outside of it) but suffers the derision of this unjust land registry. And we must admit that in our known history we have done nothing but follow the incline, degenerated from elite to elite: that we learned to predict, (miserably) to cram, to covet. That here we are neither better nor worse in the melee of interests. Lingering, moreover, in the eyes of the field of technologies where the Occident ripens its arrogance. And maybe not even raised by our derisory desires. But I proclaim that we have another destiny, another function for the world: and that we must, beyond this vow itself, this cry itself, this passion, establish with rigor and minutia the detail of our dispossessed holdings, prepare with gravity the weight of liberated sagacity in our (at long last communal) land.

And if I listen to the voice of the Occident, the greatest politics, the deepest dogmas, the most just creators, I can *hear* the silence every time it comes to this future in which to share the different abysses of man. In respect to which we are similarly new, one and other, in the new injunction. And I don't forget the phenomenal denials throughout this history of the Occident opposed, as though in prevention (: prevent, suspect, reject) of the relation. Only the poets here were listening to the world, fertilized in advance. We know what time is necessary for us to hear their voices.

Only the poets.

And I am told: What else do you do besides speak the language of the Occident? And what else to you speak of besides that which you object to? – But I don't object, I am establishing a correlation. And if I answer that, like those who do not recognize themselves as (do not feel) French and who use the French language, I must seek to sort out my business with it, I am met with the retort that I am more French than I think. For of course, once again, one is justified in revealing me to myself. (Moreover, I do not in turn retort with any recognized past, any decisive act, any irreducible crowd.) And then, if I contest thus, who am I indeed to handle the language, to weigh the concepts, to proclaim Homer or Dante? It would be preferable if I were more "authentic", and why not, more savage. Then I would be granted my difference. But my difference is in the usage I make of the concept, not in the refusal (or the impossibility) of rendering it abstract. In my manner of passionately frequenting this language, not in my ignorance of it. The Philosopher held forth on the unconscious germ and conscious maturity of Civilizations. Maybe in the modern world, with this uncertainty of begun knowledge, this weight of accumulated threats, we are living all and at once (in relation to the obligation to change ourselves – without exchanging ourselves – for the other) our conscious germ, our subconscious maturity. The germ: the known of birth, growth that watches itself grow. Maturity: the tool, the weapon, the presence of mind, the moment, liberty. Indeed we have no absolute conscience nor total power over how nor when: we make efforts to untangle the web in which the world catches us. But we are aware of consciousness: the germ knows and bears itself.

All "willful" literature today (meaning which will soon be overtaken) consciously prepares its maturity, arms language with science.

What then is language? This cry that I elected? Not only the cry, but *absence* beating in the cry.

For if you grant me through the throat Such or Such, to convince me that I must surrender,

I in turn disgorge for you the song of the one who for the night's duration rose along the cliff of acacias,

tracked from the primordial forest and from forest to forest above the sea and the oblique bridges pushing toward this morne,

and who had only known so to speak the slope the incline the loose bridge the rolling abyss the pitching morne

and who, dry toes in the mud, all night, the first, rose in the thickness of the morne,

and there launched his cry that was immediately lost in the immensity of this minuscule space,

swallowed, dwindled, eroded by the workshops, the cane fields, the violated splendor of the Unique Season (the cry),

at each crossroads each day reduced in the trivial conquest in which the other laced us,

emptied to the availability of so many good talents that we became

(when in the lair of cane the breath of slave ships turns sour),

cry to the world launched from the highest morne and un-heard by the world,

submerged there in the sweetish wave where men are limed by the sea; —

And it is to this absence this silence and this involution that I bind

in my throat my language, which thus begins with a lack:

And my language, rigid and dark or alive or strained is that lack first, then the will to slough the cry into speech before the sea.


(What does language matter, when we must of the cry and speech measure there its implantation. In every authorized lan-guage, you will build your language.)


Being, in effect, is no longer elected in the solitary resonance of a language. If the word *soleil* for certain Frenchmen has taken another meaning since Louis XIV, or the word *sea* another influ-ence for certain Englishmen after Trafalgar, I remain a stranger to that slow maturation which ends up contaminating users of language. In other words, every nation yesterday was still perfecting itself in the unique and often exclusive, aggressive projection of its parlance. But I am not heir to that unicity, having not even to react against it. Academic purifications of language are of no concern to me (neither satisfy me, nor render me indignant, nor make me smile); I am however passionate (so as not to say, oh grammarian, on the other hand) when confronting its law. For whatever may be said, the bonds of my collectivities to the cultural entity manifested by its law have been alienating. I haven't to prove my loyalty, nor continuity, but to jar it in my direction: it is my way of recognizing it.

Formerly, because of multilingualism, Swiss, Belgians or Canadians were held to be exceptions. And perhaps in effect this exceptional character granted them particularities, sometimes entailing certain kinds of cultural inhibition. There, those peoples still find spectacular pretexts for internal conflicts. To experience multilingualism at a time when each language was affirming its genius to be solitary (very often against others: the nation opposing other nations solidarily opposed to it) was not without danger or traumatisms. But today's nation is no longer "consubstantial" with a (*its*) language; multilingualism is the natural condition of a part of the world. An African child freely learns two (or even three) idioms at school and, past the time of the imposition of a language precipitating complexes, extraction, cultural sterility, this new condition opens another cycle of expression.

For if, within the information sublimated (relegated) by a language, one approached yesterday and formerly different languages, and perhaps seriated them, we should take into account that tomorrow's being will *naturally* speak several languages; that each language (each choice of parlance) will run from one of these languages to others, of course by its motivations and not within a mechanism of vocabulary (otherwise language will have been reduced to an Esperanto); that consequently the analysis of each language should integrate the study not only of concerned languages but again of *their conjugated reaction in the being*. To define a language will be to define the general attitude of the being before the words he is using, yes; but also to approach the principle (in the being) of an elocutionary symbiosis which will signify one of the modalities of its liaison to the totality of the world.

Language will then no longer be, in the expression of being, pure obstacle and pure accomplishment; it will include as well, always in contradiction, detention and relation. Poetic language will not only be approached differently than common parlance, but already as the language of a language (the latter novel in relation to several languages whose harmonious conjugation it will have achieved, and whose usage it will regulate).

Again, if language in Occidental history has been considered positivist, as a victorious realization within the norms of a closed language, how not to admit that henceforth it will increasingly nourish conscious and fecund nostalgia of the languages it *does not comprehend*: nonetheless at a more accidental level we have dreamt (those who do not know German) before Hölderlin's *The Rhine*, trying keenly, with the assistance of several translations, to enter into the mass of that text. This lack, this awareness of lack, will be necessary to consider when we want to appreciate some of modernity's languages (which will quickly become antique). Linguistics, inasmuch as it formulates constants and rules, will already find itself fallen behind the vagabondage of languages and of parlances that in each (collective) being will manifest the presence of the being in the world. It will need to pass from static analysis to dynamic profiles, if it wants to encompass this condition; short of which it will but confirm an anachronism and be jointly responsible for the blindest academic accommodations.

From this last point of view, to purge a language today (extract from it its foreign vocables) will indeed reveal itself to be less profitable than to settle the language in its giving-receiving condition (and thus formerly the nation in its relation to the Other) and work to make it overtake with real composites its historical or accidental compositions. This work could not be regented by a suspect authority. On the contrary, a certain distrust of the rhetoric of language might once more signify the deep distress of the being who refuses to share the world and words. The silence of words could reveal in the being the silence of the world. The era of proud languages in their purity must end for man: the adventure of languages (of diffracted but recomposed poetics of the world) begins.

The road is downhill to the shore, seized by the span of green, dark or light, which gathers the gaze on both sides and projects it into itself. Here and there what barely shines, what glitters and moves immobile, is the red flower. No trees or outlines are discernible. The color green, illuminated by the frail wind of the red flower. A single bound.

(When I say: tree, and when I think of the tree, I never feel the unique, the trunk, the mast of sap which, appended to others, will group together this stretch of forest cleaved by light. The European forest stole me off elsewhere: I was in the undergrowth of Hesdin as in a simplified universe where *the avenue* and perspective, in the most dense part of the thicket, were promising. But here the tree is the surge, the Whole, the boiling density. Let me try clumsily to draw a tree: I will reach a span of vegetation, where only the sky of the page will put an end to the indeterminate growth. The unique loses itself in that Whole.)

So I have only retained a few of the names that diversify these leaves. I am reluctant to seriate the names of trees, of birds, of flowers. What stands out of the mass is significant: (sugar cane); the kapok tree that at midnight eludes all vegetation to enter into the circle of ancestral powers; the acoma and the locust tree, as fallen and ravaged as the race of maroons they watched over; the arum lily, the parrot beak, sullied splendours of touristic employ; the hut poppy; several others of course, which like these are among those of our history. As for the rest, let's leave to the surge its indistinct force. What, this red flower? The flower, simply, that blows in the elevation of the Whole.

Human truths do not always burst open today in a tense flash, but evaluate themselves through the repetition, the difficult approximation, begun again each time, of a theory of obviousness (just about, of banalities) whose consciousness here and there refuses its lessons. The flash is the art of blocking obscurity in its revealed light; the accumulation, that of consecrating evidence in its duration at last perceived. The flash is of the self, the accumulation is of all. The former unfurls the absolute and unrealizable vow of the Other in being, the latter leads the relative and perfectible knowledge of relation.

The poetics of duration, in that it opposes itself, enclosing it, to the flash of the instant, authorizes a level of expression (where the poem is no longer the sole and aristocratic reservoir, the only conduit of poetic knowledge) this repositioning of smothered, deepened impositions of the relation. It suspends the imperiousness of speech, and in stages, in obscure and extracted strata, opens the being onto his lived relativities, suffered in the drama of the world. No, it doesn't reveal; it unveils with gravity. It allows for the anchoring of the unique, the particular, the flash principle of each community to the patience of its soon to be declared relationship to the Other. It arms with science those of the world who have neither science nor power; establishing that expansiveness is not exclusively of power, but tangent to a lucidity, a vocation that culminates in the vow, the call, the realization of the Other. The flash, however ardent and rich, is extinguished in the misunderstanding of the world as relation. You are only you if you accept me with active consciousness. Otherwise, you clip, you sterilize yourself. Such for the moment is the non regulated law of the universe. Before out-lasting itself, History attempts a joining of all Histories. Such is for today the vow of pressing time. Every community arms itself with receiving, when it has power to give. We will draw from the absolute felicity of the instant when, joined without exception to the multiple which everywhere wants equivalence, we will all be liberated from the lack, the misfortune, the delays, the solitudes, the injustices, the madnesses, the subconscious – (of) the Other.

I build my language out of rocks. I write, indeed, with the feeling of some scribe, like an instructor from Fort-de-France (or maybe Fort-Lamy?). But it is word-for-word my language that *instructs me*. I abuse the blissful parentheses: (it is my way of breathing). But leaving that aside; there is a more secret motion: in the poor adaptation of this language for those who had first to hear it spoken. It is that here I am confronted with this necessity to exhaust all at once the deserted (devastated) field of history where our voice has dissipated, and to precipitate that voice into the here and now, into the history to be made with everyone. Tension and obscurity result. This language is not, in its intention, approachable today by those who first should hear it: but it is also that they hear no language that is their own; their natural parlance is smothered in misery; and under the best circumstances, that is once emerged from misery, their borrowed parlance is constrained by the derision of the linguistic usage of the other. Freedom for a community is not limited by rejecting a language, but might sometimes be enlarged by building from that imposed language a free language: to create. The fetishistic respect of the imposed language contributes to sterilizing collective creative capacity: the constraining power attempts to eternalize that respect; it succeeds by the creation of a group of semi-literates whose role here is fatal. "Créolisme" for example is both the enriching of language and victory over those fronting as literate. My nation, in its duration, its breadth, its science and its savor is to be built, as is its parlance. Drama of the world. Here we are a few of us, alone with the exasperated advance of the word. Trembling with the enormous privilege of our limited knowledge. We call the future nation, and already cannot breathe without it. For it is not only State, it is for us Poetics of the being that is finding itself. We are suffocating. We are calling out for those who have no voice; but it is their parlance that supports us here. They are dying, they are *truly* suffocating. We are vomiting the literate bards: when at last our people will speak, our voice will be sure. We will dwindle isolated on our minuscule land, and we are also (we, the earth, the voiceless people, the voice of the sea) the call, the fire, the force, the vow of the world. How are we to assume the relation to the Other, when we have not (yet) any (scholarly) opacity to oppose to it, to propose? Language, here, "beginning", enlists these possibles.

The tragic joy of the world: in the secret of its modalities plays out unconscious maturity. Then, to consent to those who have no voice the "willful" conquest of their parlance: until they are able to live their parlance with ease. It is imperious to admit to each the duration of his language. What is necessary here for one and other, communities heavy with history and despoiled communities, is not in effect a language of communication (abstract, flayed, "universal" as we know it) but on the other hand a possible community (and, if possible, regular) between mutually liberated opacities, differences, languages.

(Whence, for the individual, this simple obligation: to open and to ravish the body of knowledge. To choose or to elect among the proffered. To name those he loves or has frequented.

The poets that have thus been practised, because the common language leant itself thus, we are now *discovering* them. We confer on them new meaning in the world: we pose them, not as absolute anymore, such as they perhaps dreamed themselves, but in their complementarity; in their relation to the other. One does not critique like this; one disposes of. The truth of poets wants for them to be available. We learn them; but it is the world that teaches. He who learns completes what he learns. He who frequents opens what he frequents.

By brute necessity we must start with what we know abruptly. An immediate and no less simple necessity is to abandon it in favor of elsewhere. We begin by glimpsing in what we know its deepest secret, deepest solitude, deepest purity. Reverdy or René Char. The reality of a man, the landscape of a man. (The particular). Then we enlarge as far as the universe, no longer underpinned by this real, nor secret in this landscape, but multiple and vast to all instances of the real and all landscapes that constitute the One. But the One is not an absolute; for us, today, and in the meantime, it is but the requirement of a relation of all to all. To found this relation with consciousness.

Growing from what one frequents, one comes to illuminate it, by understanding oneself; and at last tries to penetrate not only the totality (the relationship to others) but again the poetics of its relation to itself (of its relationships to this relation and to itself related). The only law to withdraw, to refuse to abolish oneself in the other, is the injunction to be integrated to the totality, to join the other there. The poets that we have frequented, we know that we must leave them here, for a more distant meeting. It is not first their succulence that we seriate, it is also their *sense* (in itself) that we reason. And we may perhaps have rallied a little of that which in itself remained spare. The relation of the relation is disjunctive and constitutive.

The language barrier falls; in such a function, language is operative. I choose or I elect: I am bricking a poem. Each language: furrow, bundle of relations atop (and within) the diverse languages and their obstacles. The poetics no longer requires the adequacy of language, but the precise fire of language. In other words: I speak to you in your language, and it is in my language that I understand you.)

*The I of the other*

# FROM THE VOW OF THE TOTAL
## TO THE SITES OF THE ONE

The existence of the Muse has always seemed to me an offense to the poet. What need did he have for a Miss thought? – But this was very much the function allotted to the Muse: to be the poet's thought, the one who prompts. It has been noted how in the Occident idealism consecrated the rupture between the poetic function and the search for knowledge. Poets were the object, roughly since the platonic idea raised itself to the sky of thought, of a banishment to which they accommodated themselves quite well. Plato had banished them from the City; what does it matter? They reserved for themselves, in the company of the Muse, the domains (without threatened borders) of sensitivity, grace, fiction, where no one tried to pick fights with them. The Occident constituted itself in the regulation of a spirituality whose most systematic intention was to isolate man, to return him repeatedly to his "role" as an individual, to confine him to himself: the methodological and technical gains thus procured hardly matter here. Thereafter, mind you, try as one might to enchant poetry with the echo of its charms, to want to reduce it to the pleasant diversity of an elected game, it was bound, in the indecision of its own purpose, to tend toward that always undecided revelation of the world, the nostalgia for which is nurtured by all. In other words poetry was denying itself at the same time as it was overtaking itself; that Ronsard illuminated Ronsard; and that in the end, haunted by a truth, provided with a delegation, the poet demanded his autonomy from science, his freedom of mien, any field to clear. With Baudelaire came the exploration of "depth", with Rimbaud the time of "Knowledge", and off went the Muse.

The latter, Rimbaud, was thus in France one of the laborers of its rebirth. *"Rimbaud the first,"* said Césaire, *"felt the nostalgia, the anguish, the modern idea of energetic forces that from within matter underhandedly stalk our quietude . . ."* In which we see that the distance is collapsed, not so much between the philosopher and the poet as between a concept and a poetics of the world. Still there was the malediction.

Not the solitude which attached itself to the poet, nor the incomprehension to which his art had destined him, but this contradiction: to move toward a total grasp of the other and the world, and at the same time to examine more and more intensely a sort of intimacy, say. Whence the satanic tension, which is one way of resolving the conflict. Rimbaud knew that this effort toward a total grasp was (in his day) premature. This is to say that his œuvre illuminated latent tendencies, that the lesson of his time was not decided, that he was a materialist with idealistic accompaniment, a poet of the world in a circle of "psychological" or descriptive poetry, and that he proposed the "Whole" while suffering the burden of a long tradition of individualism. He always desired, in the dialectic of place and of formula, to rationalize his attempt. It was to sense the precipitation of History, at the head of which he consumed himself. His malediction was to have lived with these contradictions. Overwhelmed scout of poetic advancement, instead of his high ambition for a total poetics, he nonetheless and despite himself bequeathed to many successors the romanticism (emptied in their work of "content" as of consciousness) of that malediction.

A generality: history is posed by man and imposes itself on him in modern experience as a ridgepole of the self: a "chamber" poet may well not be futile but is without a doubt incomplete; in their growing complexity "human sciences" render very approximate the conventional deepening of the psychological field on which, moreover, the opening of the world imposes a new evaluation. From there it is possible in just as banal a manner to propose regurgitated constants: sensitivity sharpens itself against knowledge, the individual is only "total" in his relation to the other, we learn (or we live) a language but meditate (or forge) our parlance. Poetry would cement (I-other, sensitivity-knowledge, nature-history, solitude-participation) the relation of man to man and to the world. But it alone cannot convoke man (with "psychologically" credulous lyricism) nor, it would seem, the world (with flattened realism).

Yet, because poetry embraces a more and more immoderate, complex, implicated (implex totality) object, does it not appear indispensable for it not to lose itself, its *intention*, in the darkness of the hypothetical call of abysses? No freedom can be founded on unpredictability, that of language less so than any other. Poetic language must guarantee a vocation of unity that poetry opposes to the dispersal of all things. That is to say once we will have realized that unity is not uniformity, and that the Total is not the Same. In a sundered world, swarming with truths, this language must be able to solicit a perennity: without which it risks being nothing more than a muddling of times: that is, in the name of some very aleatory essential-and-undistracted-knowledge, it will go so far as to lose its significance, which is to illuminate, to open a multi-reality (or rather a multi-relation between realities) to a sometimes "exploding" dynamic, which is always "fixed".

Indeed the concern for organized language must not lead to a stuffed rhetoric that cannot satisfy as first and last resort. And such a rhetoric, thinking itself the object and subject of the poem, would abolish itself in a perpetual and vain effervescence. But it is not good for example to abdicate the obligation of an apt language (which deliberately chooses to escape every injunction of consecrated rhetorical systems) in the pure and simple incapacity of ordering its language. This confusion is not always remediable. The attempt at poetic knowledge then risks escaping more and more (that is one of the "paths") from the consumed passion of the instant to inscribe itself in the attention demanded of duration: the imagination of contracted-expanded rhythms that motivate the immediate imaginary, the sensibility-knowledge that arms the sensible, the mediating history that vanquishes sudden destiny (where, for some, history that is yet "to be done" surfaces from "suffered" history).

With Rimbaud – and his kind before or after him – yes it's the Occident that solicits the world: relaying it, the deliverer was equally the abandoner. The Other that I am is implied (in its totality) in the I of this Other. But the vow of poets vanished in the bloody conquest. It will be necessary to await the combative act of the Other for the occidental I (beyond the panic of sharing and of sharing of oneself) to be able to overtake and remake itself, in a new relation.

Little more than an indiscernible revelation, poetry is not formal knowledge. The poet has legitimized his privilege to provoke the impossible (for example, the One). For, in this relation to the impossible, poetics opens onto all possible relations: at the increasingly realized approach of the condition of man in the world (for example, over totality. Totality is the possible relation that authorizes, in the tortured split distance of the world, the failed dream of the One). The poetic absolute is thus deferred to the relative each time it is conquered.

(And it seems that, to exhaust the vow of totality today by realizing the thickening of the totality of the world, man carries art toward its diffuse death; – or maybe it is there that the unsuspected capsizes?)

He was obstinate and was only the calm man we have come to know, so that he could protect his pursuit. He hasn't the flashes, the impatience of Rimbaud, but fixes his attention on the "absolute", a tension of every moment toward the consecration of the poetic dream, and maybe a pained pleasure in deferring the time line of that which could not fall to him. His obstinacy is fortified with his awareness of failure: in this awareness lies plenitude.

It is not surprising that little by little Mallarmé confused the Word and the expectation of that Word, the Book and the presentation of the Book, nor that he devoted so many obscure years to the staging of the Œuvre. The work of a poet appears (to this poet) derisory, in light of what he dreamed: it is only ever the foam of that ocean from which he wants to extract a cathedral, a definite architecture. Mallarmé is one of the few to admit to this lack, to cultivate that absence: until he makes of absence a presence, and, in some respects, of the deficiency of poetry, poetry's aim and its end.

The foam that comprises his poems (foam at the surface of the object, but gushings and fountains for us), these traces of the great stern wave could only effectively simulate deficiencies for him. More profoundly, he was implementing, ordering the Absolute, and he had agreed not to know what the Absolute might be (what it is). He exhausted himself predicting or preparing the only possible attire, and he withdrew its apparition indefinitely.

It seems to me that here perhaps lies the interest of the papers he left behind (presented and commented by Jacques Scherer): to establish in our eyes the clairvoyance of a man before the inaccessible that he senses, the heroic obstinacy of a poet preparing for an advent he knows will not take place. Pushing further is perhaps hazardous. Jacques Scherer writes: "The poetic thought we seize here at its source and even before it has arrived at a formulation . . .", which may carry a contradiction. No poetic thought is possible in the Mallarméen enterprise, other than by reference to the poem. Everything that comes *before* is illusory. It is indeed the drama, the greatness of Mallarmé, to have in the margin of the poem perpetuated the illusory, the mise en scène (because he knew the Œuvre to be an impossibility) and to have agreed to this deficiency. One could not for example assimilate the flashes of Pascal, his burning thought, to this groping, these numbers, these calculations of a man who sometimes, and with lucidity, is not writing but denying writing.

Still, Mallarmé reigns in and tenses the arc of his language. All writing meditates (or *reflects*) its own structures, its function. It happens that for Mallarmé the meditation of language effectively precedes the coming of the poem, in an active and executory manner. He doesn't only exert his poetics in the act of the poem but already in the arduous and knowing silence that precedes and prevails over it. There, there is no (not yet, or not only) poetic thought, but indeed a *poetics of thought*. Mallarmé's papers are never in this sense drafts but, say, beginnings, outlines. We also see that these "structures" of the poem, such that he arranges them or meditates them, are charged by him with a sort of negative energy. Not because he would oppose them to the rolling (and in reality illusory) fire of what will be (or might be) inspiration, but because he mixes them in the ritual as much as spiritual practice of staging the Œuvre; in other words, in my view, in an operation of which he knew he would not see the end: in an absence.

After Rimbaud had reconnected the thread of energies (relinquishing the pursuit, where he felt that time – historical necessity – hadn't fertilized place or formula), Mallarmé exposed its mechanisms (himself also relinquishing, because his *science* was not supported by the knowledge of others). Consequently, with him, a poet begins to *critique* his own formulation (his whole expectation of the poem is lucid, active, as much as it is desperate) and thus to meditate on his formula. But today and for us the place throbs consubstantially with the formula. Any science of relation is incomplete if not  bound in an earth out of which it flares – and escapes.


To claim that what is mature before the poem is illusory is thus not to reduce this *before* to a void, nor claim that the poem bursts purely forth from a sudden blossoming. The difference between the critical study of the outlines or structures of language and the same study undertaken by the poet is enlarged by the verification, at the same time (and, so to speak, sooner or later) of his purpose, which immediately becomes an *ars poetica*, in the responsible and engaging act of the poem. A poetics of thought, shared perhaps with several others, is then transfigured or not, by this engagement and according to the poem's having or not justified it as "poetic thought" proposed to all. Its intention is illuminated *in the second degree*: by stumbling or by completing itself. There, the illusion illustrates itself: failure or accomplishment. It is licit to pose the œuvre in relation to the books that comprise it (and Mallarmé's *attitude* before his language is as important for literature as is the corpus of his poems), but it is because in the global relation œuvre-intention-works the last term (the *term*: the books) constitutes the real negative of the set. Literature first addresses itself to it (history, criticism or literary dynamics): to nevertheless better reveal the global sense toward which intention strove to lead.

The Œuvre-absence is thus (yet) the only present, whose books evermore are the revealers in the negative. Mallarmé lived that tragic and magnificent imbroglio, that insupportable condition, absolutely.

In this man also this deficiency of "poetry", undetermined by the quality of man's irreducibility to the quality of poetry, but resulting for him from the feeling that the latter was called to explore domains which may not have been prohibited but arduous to conquer. It happens that one emerges from the exquisite revelation of the instant to go and decorate the wisdom of duration, that one leaves the burn of the object to reach the voice of the landscape. From the elected moment and the immediately "full" object in duration and in landscape (which root the instant and the object in their total meaning, thereby accomplishing every named-reality as a "significance") there is for Valéry the near distance of the pleasant lure to austere truth. His intellectualism is reinforced by this conviction that poetry should distance being from the pretence of the flash. "I feel each word in all of its force, for having awaited it indefinitely." Indeed he wanted not to be a poet in the – for him – archaically illuminated sense of the word. Perhaps he thus sacrificed something of grace, of fire and of the inspiration one is accustomed to lending to poets, but in the name of a higher purpose: to "draw from the self a cry as pure as a weapon." His poetic deficiency is an even more certain poetic ardor.

But Valéry was also the man of temptations. For this "amateur of poems" who went his slow way, it seemed for him more than for any other that there were moments of revelation. One night changed his universe. One letter could determine a book. Devoted to his vocation, Valéry challenged temptations, the great moments that stalked him. Perhaps his poetry encapsulates and comprehends all of this: double and troubled spectacle of a marble veined with tremors. The observation, self-motivated and scrutinizing the same purpose, merits our further attention.

Valéry was sensitive to the flight of things ("Everything flees!"), to their solitude in constant motion. This man of self-evidence knew that every substance is mobile, escapes. His fascination carries him toward the sea, the mirror, "the secret threshold of the echoes of crystal", "the laughing water, and the unfaithful dance of waves". Close to him "stone walks, and stumbles", and for him alone "those that are flowers of shadows have come". His dream would be to remain "Without speaking . . . among the obscure flowers"; but it is not possible for it not to change, not to move. He confides: "I am in you the secret change." And to complete that cry, more desperate than one might imagine: "Beautiful sky, true sky, look at me change!"

Such an insistence of terms is convincing. Valéry did not, before the substance of things, have the beautiful assurance of he who defies mysteries, who imprisons their essence and illuminates it here and now. He convinces himself in the trembling gardens that every essence trembles and capsizes. He requires time and space to know himself among things: he is the first poet, since XVIth century France, to examine a duration, to excavate a landscape. Not formally but unto its "severe essence". One understands that the essence will not be "revealed", but patiently encircled; when he catches it, it will not only be in its immediate savor, but still in its evidence and intelligibility, in its span and persistence.

This poet only considers himself knowledgeable when pressed against everything that surrounds him. A dual state – of the evidence that poses and the opacity that encapsulates, by which Valéry attempts to measure himself against the other. If he liked silence, it was for the immobile weight conferred to the landscape. "If the god sings, he ruptures the all-powerful site." Valéry's silence is neither laziness nor renunciation, but like a concentration (of glimmers). In this silence, the poet attempts to equal himself to the landscape, to endure. "Time glimmers, and the Dream is knowledge." A commentary to which one is obliged: Time, given here as duration, encapsulates and expresses itself in that glimmering ephemera par excellence: while the ephemeral of the Dream is accomplished in the permanence of knowledge. On the contrary, it is also good that some "clear song" comes to order the tumult, otherwise the tumult is in vain. Dual state of continuing reception and abrupt imposition by which Valéry wishes to survey the other.

Abandoning revelation, the naked flash, by force he enlarged the poetic instant and moved beyond the limited actuality of the object. Every substance is considered in its play and in its duration, is only pleasing by them. The "Great Hymn" of the "immense fable": Valéry intends to name being in its more knowledgeable totality. As for the landscape he might dream about, which was appropriate to the frail fixity of such a search, he did in fact know it and meditate upon it: the Mediterranean world.

The Midi has never so warranted being called Milieu, land of balance, as when one observes the duality that agitates its depths.

Those places of drought, of rigidity, of clarity, we feel a sadness there, a calm knowledge of death, an opacity that grabs hold beneath the limpidity. This sensation contributes, in certain elect places to the Mediterranean universe, with an obsessive sense of tragedy. Beneath the cut-out of shapes, this world imposes the troubled condition of man, naked among things that aren't evident. It seems that clarity only reigns there to accuse insufficient seeing. It seems that heat there is like a fog, veiling the essences. It is the place in which substance requires a call to the powers of the mind as much as the measures of the senses in order for us to approach it. It is the area of duration. There, Narcissus leans into his own image, to try to decipher the self-evidences that offer and refuse themselves all around. But Narcissus is both clarity and darkness to himself, like the trees and the beasts, like the lands and the waters that become his double.

This landscape is Valéryan. It is suited to the sought after quality: the clear form constraining the obscure density, the shiver of energies endlessly deporting the sharpness of forms, the immobility of the dream in the agitation of life. It doesn't much matter to Valéry that the word burns, even if all of language does not support the surge of being. The "severe essence" is not the naked being of things, so to speak, but an organization, a syntax of existence, that rather than be caught must be seriated. There is no single word that unveils, there is a parlance that attempts to preserve things in their end, that is, in their immediacy, in their solitude. Death as assured clarity appears as the only moment at which obviousness fully meets murkiness, where being can at last seize the other: duration includes the instant, and there it is very much the "Temple of Time, encapsulated by a single sigh."

This is sufficient indication that Valéry allocates to the poetic œuvre an unexpected significance. Himself enclosed in the injunction to consent to the instant, that he dreamed of abolishing with the clear message of a duration, he suffered for not being able to reach from here the dialectical accomplishment of the "calm roof". He envied the privilege of death, in which the double state of all things rallies in the unique wisdom of that "relay" that is eternity. Deported toward the obsolescence of a language by which he intended to preserve the precision of his intention, Valéry transports us each time his formulation opens him to the dazzling approach of the order of the world. These accomplishments are perhaps not for us the most appropriate: but (accepting the risks of the undertaking) the extreme tension with which he wanted to make of poetry a coherence, a necessity, a parlance that organized itself and didn't surge forth, a concerted surprise of the world and not amazement (precisely) without echo.

A landscape. What is that, to man? The deliberate series of an always fugitive rapport. The place, stolen off at last, whose formula trembles. Here, after Rimbaud and Mallarmé, is what in himself (in his passion for the One) Valéry conquers. *We must attempt to live.* What is a country if not the rooted necessity of the relation to the world? The nation is the expression, now grouped together and matured, of this relation. Each time the nation is oppressed, there is a height of plenitude between itself and the land. When, on the contrary, the nation tyrannizes the other, dominates the earth, misunderstands the world as consenting relation, it denatures itself. For which certain men under certain circumstances choose their country over their nation. Every poetics *of our day* signals its landscape. Every poet, his country: the modality of his participation.

(And it seems that this agony or this death of art are joined in an exhaustion of forms saturated with unicity; and that the surprise of the world (the unsuspected) must be infinitely multiplied – in the stellation of these infinite landscapes).

# PURE LANDSCAPES

For him, no "concept of the world", no body of doctrine, no tyrannical system implicating its environs. Is this to abdicate the so-called powers of poetry, to wean poetry from its ambition to illuminate? Is it to return it – naively and falsely crude – to a state of pure poetry? Is it to mummify it with sentiment and confession? Reverdy replies: "It is no longer a matter – today it is a given – of eliciting emotion through the more or less pathetic exposition of a news item, but as broadly, as purely as possible, at night, by a sky crackling with stars, the calm, grand, tragic sea,  or a great mute drama played by the clouds beneath the sun." First, a refusal, now generalized, to resort to the tricks of the "daily news"; and this refusal, the poet outfits it, so to speak, with sombre serenity, with solitude. This tragedy is calm, and this drama, mute: here does Reverdy's part begin. How far does this solitude extend? It seems at first to exclude men, leaving the poet free to penetrate immediate life: objects and materials, skies and trees. Reverdy is a visionary of the concrete.

One enters into this œuvre as into a second nature, acting according to its eternal nature, and whose motives seem to depend closely on the cloud's mood or on the forest's, on the landscape's "temperature" , or on the streets' efflorescence. Still, Reverdy is solidly attached to a clear concept of the domains of poetry. "Nature is nature, it is not poetry. It is nature's reaction in the complexion of certain beings that produces poetry." For which these beings dream of establishing (igniting or illuminating) close contact with the forces of the universe. Not the cosmic forces, the unleashing of the Whole, but the humble and tenacious current of sap that in each thing accomplishes itself. And man may want to elicit this contact (despite the density countered by the real), because nature corresponds to the mind – by its simple truth, according to Reverdy; as it would correspond, according to Claudel, with the obligation "offered" to every creature to be co-born with the world and of itself. "Nature is complicated. Such an entanglement of lines, of forms, of colors. But as it is true, it corresponds to the mind with simplicity." Reverdy will articulate his poetics from this proposition. The œuvre will be the *natural field* in which it will have arranged to meet men (a meeting to which they are of course not obliged): the poet is that emotion-carrier of the human, capable of maintaining the "effervescent contact of the mind with reality". Reverdy is no less aware of the aforementioned density, of the real's resistance to investigation. He receives a diffuse despair from it. Here the contact must be sought, the point of impact (maybe a warm contamination), not a total and impossible communion. Here is the poet: "Apparently a prisoner, cramped in this world, otherwise purely imaginary, which the commoner accommodates, he overtakes its obstacle to reach the absolute and the real; there his mind moves about with ease." – And here is his power: "By choosing only what is constant and permanent and the true substance of things, art claims today to feed only from the real and to reach this reality which fixes the work of art and enables it to take place among things existing in nature."

No dependency in relation to nature; art chooses and purifies: in that resides its liberty and the power of the mind. Next, the real is not combined with that appearance which we have accommodated for so long (the absolute that qualifies it is "constance and permanence": hidden beneath – and against – fluidity of forms.) It is moreover not a matter either of submitting to nature or of profiting from it, but, through the poem, of granting it a sort of nurturing catalysis: in this will (or that deaf desire) to re-do, through the poem, the Moderns are noticeably different from the *Naturalists* of the old poetics. Finally, this last ambition posits the poem as a thing which, created, also responds densely to the laws of existence and of duration as this tree or this plain. Neither a realist nor a mystic, since here it is possible to be a visionary without being a mystic, Reverdy is an undertaker of the concrete. But how does one carry out this art that is "an eminently terrestrial thing". One cannot help but stumble against the obstacle, the torment without end, which is also its only weapon: the word. For Reverdy, obstinately concrete, how is he to use such an abstraction as the word?

He *densified* the word. The latter, abandoned to its own devices, maintains balance in its own space (the page), lives off its surly existence. For the most part, Reverdy's first poems are organized according to obscure laws of gravitation. Each cluster (word or line or group of lines) signifies its world, and if it encounters, in the clusters that accompany it, the plenitude that makes of the poem a unit, that relation nonetheless altogether escapes syntactical or "sense" logic, to go foremost toward a near-vital correspondence. The nakedness (apparent poverty) of language makes this cartage more sensitive. Thus allocating to the word a vocation of concreteness, the poet lives on watching live (living with) realities that words cover over, symbolize.

> *The stream cries coming down the street*
> *The prisoner trees listen quietly to one another,*

> along this same trail that continues to climb

> *up to the bloody rock where the light perishes . . .*

No one can really densify (concretize) words; other than, like Reverdy, through wanting to establish between them uncanny relations, a syntax of plenitude or of emptiness, spaces and attractions. A desperate attempt, indeed, that can only be sustained by the poetic absolute experienced to the point of asceticism. Yes. This poet is also an ascetic of the concrete. Having escaped the temple of books (*And all of these great ideas no longer move; they sleep, or are dead*) there, outside, the man rediscovers the immanence of things, which solicits and includes him.

> *To detach the mind from this same story*
> *We must walk directly without condition*
> *Toward the more real life.*

Weighted and deaf work, exploration of the depths. And the poem "must rise, painfully, from below". To experience the world. Neither reminiscence nor transcendence: "actuality". Whence this observation that the poems of Reverdy are as many tableaux, pure acts, *presents*. His offering is the antithesis of the lucid absence in which Mallarmé isolates himself. His rhetoric will be contrary as well: not that of a harmoniously tight scheme, but a trajectory open to dullness. The offering of the concrete becomes a means for knowledge, by which the poet discovers for the other the paths of the real; for which perhaps "this need to express that characterizes him comes to him, not always clearly, of the superabundance of *being* that he carries within." The being shudders at remaining closed, immobile, left to his own devices; isolation is lack, the distress against which he must struggle every day. Yet what the being wants to reach moves intensely in turn, escapes, "everything is always up and ready to go"; a man remains riveted, stagnant in the full of that shuddering becoming,

> *Waiting for something to happen*
> *Who knows what.*

The task then is to fix movement, errant (muttering) life, we must seize "the ball's bounce". Leaving man to his isolation, things flee, are moved or appeased. But the truth is there, in man's fixation on the concrete. At least in the open attention he grants it. Pure landscape. In the end, through the arduous, deliberate exercise of his vision, the being forces his blindness. He accommodates himself to the real. His universe organizes itself. He has not only tried to *draw the real to him*, to humanize the substance for lack of being able to substantiate human expression; in his relation to the real, he has not simply transferred his affection to things. He has built a world, analogic (and not repetitive) of the world. Illusory and convincing world. Relation, and not mass; but an operative relation: livable. The word risks its significations, becomes parlance: the poem is no longer simply a pure offering, it calculates its own chances:

*Because evening has passed*
*space is traversed*
*the moon as it comes down to look*
*has stopped*
*And face to face I watch deep in the eye*
*What is happening*
............................
*There are but a few muddled words left in the last stirrings*
  *of the chest*
*The trap has sprung*
*The dream lighting comes on*
*Memory delivered*
*Sorrows lost in the air*
*Overtaken borders*
*All the ties untangled beyond the seasons take their turn again*
  *and their tone on the dark backdrop of silence*

The silence of a man whose work has been profitable. Equilibrium, despite the "muddled words". The poet has passed from
isolation among all things to a sort of lesson of things; there is an
ethics there.

The attachment to the concrete raises these powers, "universal"
and very secretly individual. By the communion it assumes with all
that exists (even if communion is forever impossible), and by the
demands it places on man to be alone in the total drama, to try to
equal it. Each is free to hear poetic parlance as he wants to; each in
effect leads his landscape from the interior: how does one propose
a uniformly receivable parlance to these carriers of different landscapes? Ethics of solitude, but *common ground*, there outside.

It is by the star, the street, the suns each time new, the natural or created things, that Reverdy joins his likeness. An encounter founded on the dark difficulty with which each is faced to arrive at the clarity of surrounding lives, and on the possibility allotted to the poet to be the one who opens the way for all. Poetry takes on a meaning and a scope, in that (which was its secret intention, regained after a good many detours) it allows each to confront his landscape (his *way of seing*, of which he may only have had a muddied awareness) and that of a man (the poet) who approached these very tight visions of the concrete and the most certain expressions of these visions.

Reverdy is one of our measures in the approximation of the real. If he himself failed in a sort of totalization of his real (if, out of necessity, the real escapes the clutch of the word), and if as a poet he carries the mark of some bitterness, this bitterness is only his (only for him) because for us he opens one of our windows onto the quotidian, a skylight (as he would say) onto the world. The absolute by which he suffered engenders for us this possible light. Beyond the poetic pleasure he procures security is born with the surroundings, even in the very place where solitude sprouts and the burst of that concern will have constrained arid isolation.

Another silence, another richness. To tell all (all told) with René Char. To quote him is to evaluate him: he is alone, and what a pure landscape. I comprehend – I mean that I love to know – this landscape (its nature), in that with him I frequent my own. The other is not others, but my consenting difference. Others are but of morality; in the Other everything is a poetics.

("Man of rain and child of good weather, your hands of defeat and of progress are for me of equal necessity.")

His poetry, at the moment at which it is most intensely present, is passionate calculation, as much as the chance, for a future. Then does it array itself with incandescent rigor as well as a threatened shiver. The rigor is of the poem, which holds an attributive force, in all senses. *Fragility and disquiet*: the suspension between a pessimism knotted to the present and that series of sparks and vibrations the future already holds.

The actual and the sensible – the terminated – which is also the threatened – only approach – and protect – one another – in their projection: in knowledge each time beginning.

("On the crests of our bitterness, the dawn of conscience advances and deposits its silt.")

It is difficult to disassociate a properly "poetic" body and a complementary sector of "ideas". The will to knowledge and accomplishment is sealed to the way of the poem. (Poetic research determines and governs the life of the mind).

Like in that countryside where "there were but filaments of wings, the desire to cry out, flutter between transparency and light", in the œuvre there quivers a question (disquiet: man's awareness of his isolation), that throbs, the same under so many formulations: to know how man will find that truth (that purity) again whose landscape bears witness here, and an answer, ceaselessly engaged, always revivified by the poetic exercise.

The two movements of poetry (disquiet-question and answer-disquiet) interfere in a spattering dynamic. Organic logic, as though needled by the echo of that hope, which resonates in fragility itself.


("O you, rainbow of this polishing shore, bring the ship close to its hopefulness. Make of every supposed end a new innocence, a feverish fore-ward for those who stumble in morning heaviness.")

The answer is in innocence: the rebirth to the world. When *The Shark and the Gull* ("Yesterday nobility was deserted, the olive branch was far from its buds. The shark and the gull did not communicate") meet at last.

Innocence is knowledge, consequently always uncertain. At least it is not gaping naiveté.

So many sharks have eaten so many gulls. The poet knows it. Yet it was night. There is no night for the work of Char (except for the night of the Résistance, in *Feuillets d'Hypnos*), there is but dawn and morning. This is a deliberate choice of his poetics. It is necessary to overtake the night, always menacing and secreting bitterness, knowing also that the time of the full day has not yet come. Dawn is the natural median, the dwelling of poetic hope. Between shark and gull how (by what, by whom) do we communicate?

("How long will the dying man's lack last at the centre of creation because creation has dismissed him?")

By the share, within being, of nature. Dangerous vocation, which risks slicing itself into the most summary symbolism. We know romantic error, according to which the landscape was especially the *consenting setting*. There is also a realism-of-purity of fields and greenery. The pastoral lurks. And in truth this is normal, for the one for whom the topic of spring and field has ancestral significance. Being is subject to simple temptation; and it is just. For example, in the poem of *Donnerbach Mühle*: "November of mists, hear beneath the wood the bell of the last trail cover the evening and disappear . . .". We might have seen there, in the text's perfection, the beginning of a poetic description (of nature) that could have sufficed without pushing further, — if suddenly other elements hadn't intervened, of another category, and which persuade us that the intention is more profound:

("Toll of an overloved world, I hear the monsters trampling an unsmiling ground. My vermilion sister is in sweat. My furious sister calls to arms.")

The poet's first act is to defend the landscape. To raise himself against its suppression by men: thus against the ignorance and formal exile in which men maintain themselves. And that René Char undertook a struggle to preserve his Provence from the nuclear scourge, that is one of those poetic necessities, the absurdity, the inoperativeness of which in the eyes of lucid people, is of the logic of a being led to his ultimate flamboyancies. Life enlarges itself by such *distances*.

In nature is the secret of innocenting forces. In it, in being, *and in their relation to one another,* that "*internal* justice", out of which a knowledge wells. Solidarity with the landscape is militant by design.

("...I glimpse the day on which several men will undertake without subterfuge the voyage of the energy of the universe. And as fragility and disquiet feed off poetry, upon their return, these high voyagers will kindly be asked to remember.")

The poet will have taken care beforehand to indicate that the future convoked here is not confined to the sole dimension of *improvement.* The communion that he summons is not altogether that of the men who organize their City. He himself confided his "indifference to history" and his love of the harvest.

Energy. ("*The energetic forces.*") It is not a "principle", nor residue; it is not that Idea that is placed behind things to bring diversity back to the comfortable unitary ideal. No, infinitely, it is a disquieted urge and often ravaged toward the conciliation of that which has so many times been opposed in man by the dissecting forces of fixed thought. And it is once again a relation to establish: "In poetry, it is only from communication and the free disposition of the totality of things between themselves and through us that we find ourselves engaged and defined, on the verge of obtaining our original form and our convincing properties." To set departure in exigency and the absolute, and the return toward us among things. "*You will be a portion of the savor of the fruit.*" The boldness of the option is itself approached: the aim of the effort and its act.

(But, so far from the history of men, who is this *likeness* of whom you spoke to us, oh poet?)

("Man flees suffocation.")

In infinite dimension, man seeks ease and plenitude (felicity). Because poetry perfects that which is incomplete, prompts the creation of that which doesn't exist (in the grace of "magical and subversive forces of desire"), it converges in that "completely satisfying presence" in which the "inextinguishable uncreated real" spreads through the being.

By which fraternity prepares itself. But Char dreams of a force other than solidarity. We die in ourselves, prisoners of our sheathing. Others are always beyond. Let us *impose* the present. Cry out that each relation to things opens onto the possible relation to the other: "The evasion in his likeness, with immense poetic perspectives, will perhaps one day be possible."

But what is this likeness, oh poet?

Will we not be able to avail ourselves of the steppes, the bush and the sands near the "tender lime" and the "starry orchard"? Will we not recognize likeness in so many others abolished in the same? Will we not affirm the irreducible alterity of likeness, for the beauty, at last realized, of evasion? Will we not clear the ground of history, to weed so many trails on which the other made his way, covered over by the nettle of ignorance?

("Shifting, horrible, exquisite earth, and heterogeneous human condition seize and qualify one another mutually. Poetry pulls itself from the exalted sleep of their shimmer.")

This relationship of language to the reality of existing things. The impossible maintained. One day we may not distinguish (other than for knowledge) what creates from what is created, living man from the living universe. The poem reaches toward that indistinction which is not confusion but synthesis (it announces it absolutely and renders it each time possible); and the synthesis in turn is neither interlace nor mechanism, but projection and maturation forever postponed. Thus the poem consumes itself in that future. At the same time as it approaches its speech, it destroys itself ("*for having said it for us*"). Like that "nomadic spark that dies in the fire", its object devours it. Eternally at the limit of the unspeakable, (even when it magnifies the present) it is foremost every appetite and stump of the future.

("Magician of insecurity, the poet has only adoptive satisfactions. Cinders always recommenced.")

As with the poet. *The excluded and the fortunate*. Man of the present, in that he claims, protects and perhaps perpetuates the actual and, despite the distances, the sheathings, which exclude him, plunge him into totality. In totality dreamed, where the outline of the landscape and the threatened freshness of its eternal tomorrow shiver together. In totality lived, where opacity opens little by little and sharing is established. Man of the future (by which we finish where we began), for the impossible of intention to enlarge itself without end on the possible secreted there: "With each collapse of proofs the poet answers with a salve of future."

("And the one who knows how to see the land come to fruition Is not moved by failure even though he has lost everything.")

The earth is that supreme argument (whose "return to the earth" was sometimes its miserable caricature). Claudel binds in the earth the apostrophe addressed to *La Muse qui est la Grâce*. Césaire, in the *Cahier*, wishes himself earth, and tree (son of earth). Man is indeed given to the future, because, a poet, he cannot here fulfill his wish; so he presents himself in his earth: it becomes (it is) the eternal wager, behind so much rich furtiveness, whose aroma is never enclosed. It is the poverty in which he nourishes himself. But the earth is different to each. There are so many lands: totality results (much more than their sum) from their relation to come. It is not possible to conclude.

At this moment when they carry their gaze to their harvests, we must leave the poets (and those who with them and in their fields will be reapers and behind them, gleaners), to clear our own ground.

(In them, that *ancient alchemy* by which, from each solitude the aura of the others becomes ecstatic. From the pure landscape, the calls of the lands. From secretion, blossoming. At the edge of the total world they express the One which aspires to the Universe.)

FROM THE ONE TO THE UNIVERSE

Such an adventure is not arbitrary: but signifies a general movement of disorientation, by which Europe, for the last two centuries, seeks to exceed its limits and its norms. There is a bit of Cook and a bit of Chateaubriand in the great voyagers; the one who discovers and the one who bears feeling. For Ségalen, he does not encounter islands but monuments of archeology; he does not intend with great solemnity to impart to his era a new sensibility, but he will imbue himself almost in secret in an altogether other way (integrated in the tradition of a people of traditions – in China) to feel and to know. He prepares and permits proud pilgrimages, thus Perse's *Anabase*, more distant, more resolutely founded on occidental anchorage. In this way, there is a privileged moment, a sort of accomplishment: when the Voyager is no longer trailed by ghosts, ceases to attend to his torments. On the road that extends from Chateaubriand's regulated enthusiasm through Perse's disengagements to Leiris's lucidity (all bound, however, to find elsewhere the shadow of what they will become), Ségalen marks, against the persistence of his being, the point of genuine deracination, of systematic denial; by which he will know, in the consumed substance of his mind and the exhaustion of his body (which will be the death of him), that he was not from Peking but from Brest, and not Chinese from the Old Empire but French from the beginning of the century.

*("Spontaneously I did something altogether else.")*

This apprenticeship of the self, adorned by such abandon to the other, could but decorate a poetic alchemy. Only poetic notation is good for composing the Journal of those Voyages, which are one of the modern forms of mysticism. Ecstasy is on display here, and conscious: it is no less extreme: the individual comes out of himself, to know the god he carries inside. For man, this god is the Other, the Foreigner, the Unknown Force; without ceasing to be the Same, the Knowable, the Intimate. Ségalen is thus exemplary: for having fully attempted to be the Other; for having accomplished the Same. If geography, archeology, ethnography appear as dogma, for the new riches of this religion without religiosity, poetry provides the Book, the Genesis and the Enumeration. Ségalen contributed to the dogma, and gave a chapter to the Book; but he did not succumb to the temptations that stalk the nomadic Solitaries of which we speak. For he did not smother the Other beneath the weight of the Same, nor inversely: his desire was the total realization of the Other in the Same (and that in itself was an original approach): he did justice to exoticism, as the detestable and anarchic movement of an exasperated sensibility toward other places.

But also, and perhaps in order to discredit the accidental-exoticism ("neither colonies nor negro souls, neither camels, nor vessels, neither great waves, nor odors, neither spices, nor enchanted Isles, nor incomprehension . . ."), he tries to constitute Exoticism into a value. A value accredited by each being's faculty to "feel the Diverse and recognize its beauty"; founded on "the knowledge (*for everyone*) that something is not itself", and on the line borrowed from Jules de Gauthier, according to which "each being that conceives itself, conceives itself necessarily other than he is". It is necessary to approach the poet through the examination of some of his theses on a subject that was absolutely *his own*: this analysis of his ideas opens onto his poetics. The Exoticism-Aesthetic of the Diverse, clear-cut theory of the narrow exotico-historical conjuncture, authorizes without denaturing the succulent *accidents* that perfect poetry. And similarly, the progression of these ideas through the century will be explained by the rustling silence first stretched around this œuvre, followed by the rebirth from which it benefits today.

("*Only those who possess a strong Individuality can feel the difference.*")

Despite Ségalen's imperative note against "boring syntheses", I persist in understanding his work as an effort toward stability ("the star is intimate and the instant perpetual"), a protestation against the "dilapidated vacillation" from which the Chinese Empire suffers, and thus Knowledge. There are for him two extreme signifiers in all things taken together: the Opposite and Likeness; two poetic constancies: the carnal and the solemn; two styles: the quotidian and "this which has no echo among other languages and would be of no use to daily exchanges". Here Exoticism finds its importance; by delousing it of passementeries and transcending it, Ségalen risks electing it as a catalyser of opposites. From what was once historical incident, he draws out a foundation for being. In truth it is not in his *Notes* that this attempt appears in its richest light (for there thought is diffuse and in some respects the skin of the word), but in the part of the œuvre that is related directly to China. *Stèles, Peintures, Équipée*. The foreign, which, in the China Ségalen chose for himself, is that of the *Stèles*, the millennial and the eternal, confronts the Pareil that, in himself, is poet, the flesh and succulence of the instant. He then reaches the ideal conditions of his adventure. Afterwards, touristic or literary exoticism are no longer possible, but the sole writing of the poem that fixes the teachings of the struggle "against limits". This tension toward a Knowledge and this attempt to perpetuate never deteriorate into obsessive imperatives: Ségalen stops, and exploits. The value of the Diverse is in its succulence; whence the poetics that is, yes, a theory of profit, of enrichment (and like these words, here, are not in the least provocative!) "If the savor grows in accordance with difference, what could be more savory than the opposition of irreducibles, the shock of eternal contrasts?" The poet is knotted to the drama of the concrete. Likeness and its opposite, though they distance themselves continually, are nonetheless fortified one by the other: "It is by Difference, and in the Diverse, that existence is exalted."

("*Before leaving the Empire to meet his soul, from Here, he arranged for his departure.*")

In the three combined and cited books, Ségalen marked, not the whole trajectory, the progression of intention, but its apogee, its glorious final literality, sometimes tempered by a certain nostalgia: the feeling of the irreducible limits of the known.

We acknowledge that the book of *Stèles* is in this regard the most important. These steles encountered on the roads of China are the most exact possible representation, in the order of material, of the poet's conceptions. They are foreign, millennial, stable, hieratic, indifferent; yet they attest to, live, support the passer-by. The stele rises, "epigraph and carved stone", soul and body: meeting place. Ségalen imbued this symbol with reconciliation and the unification of the diverse; he had been designated to love this eternity of form, its majesty. He didn't want to describe those steles, but to provide a poetic equivalent; ". . . on the scale, by degrees of artifice, of the arts, is it not one notch higher, to speak one's vision, not crudely, but by an instantaneous, constant *transfer*, the echo of one's presence?" We could not reproach Ségalen an academic symbolism nor a realist re-presentation. His poetry recomposes, and does not weaken from the tenor imposed by his project: to signify distancing in presence itself.

Blazing or frozen, language maintains itself then at the extreme tip of speech. Ségalen despises what is tepid ("tepid paste"), as much as he execrates abandon. His lyricism might be tense if it weren't immediately nourished by the flavors of the real. There, in effect, lies its flash: such rigor in refusal, that mastery bordering on aestheticism; then (at the same time) the delights of the eye ("vision, skies") the subtleties of the mind, irony, and a manner of familiarity ("the *tu* will dominate") that creates distance as surely as the pomp of the classics.

*Thus, without stopping or stumbling, without halter or stable, without merit or sorrows, you will reach not, friend, the marsh of immortal joys*

*But the eddies full of drunkenness of the great river Diversity.*

The intimate (ornament, and to all, the *delicious accident*) introduced by this language of annunciation, only made itself sensitive after a sort of *reprise*: first it was "masked" by the *vision* of the poem and by the theory of those Steles. Where it is a matter of betrayed friendship, or of the flash of a "Savage oath":

> *Do not rely on any member of your clan to settle this affair: you*
> *or I or both of us killed, — this, I swear:*
> *By these two great dogs with tawny fur, crucified there back to*
> *back!*

Whether it is a familiar game, lucid irony, or Decrees of the Emperor, a love song ("My mistress has the virtues of water"), or Peking, *Purple prohibited city*, — the measure of the verb, without confusing and muddling its maps, imposes an architecture of the stele, "being in completion". Deeper in, it is yet but "that unique era, without date and without end, with unspeakable characters, which every man installs in himself and salutes",

> *At dawn when he becomes Sage and Regent of the throne of his*
> *heart.*

The descriptions of the *Peintures* and the landscapes in *Équipée* complete the setting of immemorial China, which Ségalen wanted to build around him and, with rare instinct, and whose central motifs he chose down to the finest details. Thus is the world of the poet accomplished.

*("The object disputed by those two beasts – being and a word – remain proudly unknown.")*

Yes, the world has remained secret. The œuvres of Ségalen knew the destiny of the *Stèles*: "Accessible to all, they reserve their best for a few." The *publicity* each wishes for them does not seem to have entered the zone in half-shadow that cloaks them. Ségalen, more than any other, is forever imbued with dull nostalgia, which isolates him. The exercise of his art is abutted by a profoundly melancholy thought, which will consume him. "The Diverse diminishes. There lies the great earthly danger. It is thus against this decline that we must struggle, fight – die perhaps with beauty." Meticulous vow of poetry. Is it not to draw from the perishing of all things their savor and their succulence? That is where, with Ségalen, we must return. He offers savor; he admits, without inconvenient abandon, his throbbing concern.

(But the Diverse is even more threatened when it is not diversely assumed: included in a plurality of beings. Its truth is that it cannot collect *the whole* of itself into one alone. Perhaps in effect after having experienced the call of the Diverse with lucidity, Ségalen was left to re-verify *his own soil*. The Diverse is only given to all as a relation, not as an absolute power nor a unique possession. The Diverse is reborn when men diversify themselves concretely in their different liberties. Then it only requires the renunciation of the self. The Other is in me, because I am me. Similarly, the I, from which the Other is absent (abstract), perishes. Rimbaud, between his Ardennish family or the Parisian littérateurs (Others, denatured) and his idea of a Red-skin or Negro (the absent Other) chooses silence (and perhaps, by obscure vengeful logic, colonialist trafficking: *you were not at my appointment, you are therefore worth exploiting*). Outside of totality (the realized, normalized relation of the Other to the Self), the Diverse vanishes. Ségalen lived too early for his vow. Innumerable are the martyred men who die today so that their Difference might be consensual, so that the Diverse may be reborn *in reality*. He might perhaps have been close to them, or supported their struggle).

(". . . *To reach the other, the fifth, centre and middle – who is in me.*")

At the heart of the œuvre, the publication of *Stèles, Peintures, Équipée.* Really and in all senses of the term the *Stèle du Milieu* ("the *lieu* par excellence",) soul and body of the Ségalenian œuvre. At once savor, torn from things, and the harmonizing of the solemn Services.

The allegation of two reasons in favor of the renewed popularity this œuvre is enjoying may not seem inopportune. One, altogether external, is that the exoticism, against whose most hateful form Ségalen struggled, tends in effect (in this form) to disappear, swept away by the implacable fury of "modernity". Thus we learn to make distinctions between the last exotics (Loti, Farrère, Ségalen), the former having resisted the shock of *elsewhere*, had quite a "strong Individuality." Cut off from such obsolescence by bloody realities, or turned toward other poles of attraction that Ségalen had anticipated (the poles, cold exoticism: the planets, extraterrestrial exoticism), the "public" assigns to each of these voyagers – Americanist, oceanist or Orientalist – the importance, ridicule, hate or pathos he deserves. The other reason, more literary, is that Ségalen's œuvre, by just return, benefits from the audience accorded to writers such as Claudel and Saint-John Perse who are read alongside the author of *Stèles*; and this without having to look for the commodity of "classification". As far as he wanted to be and as close as the closest inhabitant, Ségalen astonishes by the force of the solitude that was his. Stubborn in his devastation, like Rimbaud, like Lautréamont: we now know that he suffered from a similar malediction. The vow of the world was in him, in him also, who was, he too, *ahead of* the world.

"And what is most essentially lacking in the individual if not being total?"

(Snickers, storms and furor, gossip, impoverishments. So much pettiness, spiritual extortions, contradictions, that are ransomed by the passion to write, we could barely understand them in Claudel, let alone succeed in "situating" them, if perhaps we didn't experience these divergences as the testimonies of a drama that plays itself here between vocation and faith. The justification of the act of writing, before the essential act of adoration that is given to faith, grants the poet wrenching obligations. From one to the other he must find the link. For prayer is not writing's creation but the reading of an already revealed Scripture. Claudel will attempt to impose faith as a condition of poetic writing, to confer necessity, in the face of God, to a poetic universe. Whence the minutia of his *Art poétique*, which must, incidentally (because this is to simplify it excessively), be followed literally in order to better understand its leap; whence also the Claudelian poem's turn against itself. The poet postulates the existence and value of a logic of the poem, capable of reassuring him. It is not surprising that he took on every reference system that did not presume the imperial foundation of poetry.

Since science is the most solidly constituted body of knowledge in the world, Claudel first tackles the mechanism of scientific laws: "(This whole mechanism) . . . the "laws" deduced from them, are but instruments of critique, points of simplification, means of intellectual assimilation. They haven't in themselves any generative force and obligatory value."

Reducing scientific intention to this mechanical, unquestioning project that it has surpassed, Claudel (thus "situated" without realizing it himself) demands that we push further ahead: where is the generative force, where is the principle of this machine that is the world? "Every machine, living or made, finds its feed and its object outside of itself . . . Yet the Universe is total and by your postulation there is nothing external to itself. What then is this force deprived of a source, this machine that feeds itself and produces itself?" (And here we recognize a sublimated version of Voltaire's somewhat impoverished "watch without a watchmaker". Enough, in this rapprochement, to bring a shudder to intransigent Claudelians.)

Let us not stop at appearances, phenomena or workings; *let us delve into things*. "Man thought that all things at all hours and with his approval belabored by the same inspiration that measures his own growth were elaborating a mystery that needed to be apprehended . . ." That *same inspiration* explains how essential knowledge does not at all *separate*; all surfacing, all growth is equivalent to an acquisition of the mind. "I call knowledge proper yes that necessity for the whole to be a part: firstly. Secondly, this part, man's freedom to *do* it, to create his own position over the whole; and thirdly this repercussion, which is to know what he is doing."

What law governs this "essential" determinism, this free will, this knowledge of man's? According to what logic is what is born organized, what enters into the "whole"? Not according to the narrow logic of scientific determinism; as for the cause, it is but total, and "every particular cause is but a fiction for our convenience." The logic of what is born is already inscribed in this vast design of the whole, which has each being arrive at their right place. No being can therefore be self-sufficient, can know himself without knowing – and being born to – the whole: "To know is to be: that which is missing from all else."

Such logic displaces the "old" which was based on syllogism, and whose organ was the metaphor. "The metaphor is the indigenous art of all that is born." Where the old logic could only be applied to appearance, to phenomenon, to "pure mathematical fact", this one interests being in itself, in the necessity for being. Claudel will strain to elect poetry as *doing* par excellence, by which man creates "for himself his position in the whole". Thus poetry, the domain of metaphor, will be installed at the heart of knowledge. The logic of what is born is in the end an *Ars poetica*.

The unity of the Whole has as its consequence the obsolescence of dualisms. The realities of the mind and of matter, "if they are radically heterogeneous, separated to their core, how could they be born one to the other, and know one another, not knowing one another? We must therefore refuse them not their difference which is fecund, but a natural isolation which is inconceivable." These two realities are implied in their participation in the Source, the Laborer of the total machine, God. And their meeting is accomplished in a sort of Being-not-Being, the Movement that precedes them. Movement "is a spontaneous act and the very instrument of existence . . . Matter and mind have this in common, that these two realities are subject to movement."

Spiritualist systems (all the more mystical) that strive to explain the world call up this dynamic and subterranean notion of motion. "For the key to the cosmic secret, writes Hans Urs von Balthazar in his *Cosmic Liturgy*, is still motion, or more precisely, it is the study of the relationship between rest and motion, whose balance is what defines the essence of finite being." And we read in the fourth poem of Milosz's *Ars Magna*: "Motion precedes the thing that is in motion. Motion, matter-space-time, is already the thing. And yet it precedes the thing . . . Space-time is not the space of motion; it is its creation, its matter. We know of no other matter than space and time. The universe, from alpha to omega, is matter. It is matter, not in opposition to the mind – a miserable human concept – but very much because it is itself thought, in other words motion."

The parts of the whole know one another in completeness and in relation, their unity is dynamic: the notion of motion authorizes the overtaking of "natural isolations", and allows for the uniform ascension of the everything toward the divine. Here then is the soul of the machine that has God as its Source.


For the poet, knowledge will no longer impede *immediate contact* with the world. On the contrary: knowledge of things is knowledge of the self as a function on the one hand and on the other hand a condition of the Ensemble. Through sensation and motion, "man constitutes himself wherever he is, he enjoys the faculty of transporting this centre wherever he wants . . . Man, by the sole fact of his existence *here*, becomes the point of coordination of diverse phenomena to which he brings his common testimony. He explains them, he attunes them, he *knows* them by his presence alone". But also: ". . . we know things by granting them the means to exert an action on our *motion*". And at last: "Knowledge comes from ourselves, it is the reading at all times of our position in the whole: intelligence is among the things we know." A poetic postulate. Not only first life, action and reaction, but (active, shared, allotted) knowledge as well are conducted in this unity of the Whole.

Yet man is not his own end. His only certainty rests precisely on the assurance of being unable to understand that which is all Existence, God. "The universe is but a total manner for not being what is . . . God alone is what is." The freedom to be is de-finite, it perfects and abolishes itself in the function that has befallen man, to be the witness and the seal of the world. Thus, man does not fulfill his service if he is closed to the world. But, as a participant of the world, he is, in everything, in relation to God but the "delegate of external relations, the *representative* and the foundation of power." In this sort of State or general Company, the representative does not, however, emanate Directorship: participation in the divine does not implicate a conjunction of substances but the necessary relation between Existence, which is God, and that manner of being that which is not Existence, which is the world. The world finds its reason and the obligation toward unity (of its poetics) precisely in this relation to Existence.

Von Balthazar writes again: "The more God is seen, in fact, as Wholly Other, the more the intellect must give up hope of reaching him by means of a "heavenly ladder" built from the steps of the created universe—and the more the world must close in on itself, in order to become in its totality, not simply in its most noble parts, a place to praise and serve the Infinite One."

It is not possible then to detach from the whole any of its parts, nor to separate the mind from matter, nor to cut man from the world, nor to divide the known from the knowing. This correspondence between all things that always haunts poets is affirmed here in the name of Christian spirituality. Claudel will carry such a detail to the extreme. Poetry is the motion by which man displaces the relations between things, knows them and *totalizes* them. The poem is the immediate contact, knowledge of things, and knowledge of the self. It participates in the real, it *comprehends* man by his surroundings, and inversely. Claudel wants to rediscover drive, an exaltation of being toward the world, that Christianity had lost. He is the Christian poet who tempted the Adventure and undertook the "voyage of the Universe."

With maniacal tyranny (for him it is a matter of life and death, of the right to speak or the obligation to be silent) he imposes the following postulate: that it is necessary to know – to sing – this world, in order to climb toward God. "Our occupation for eternity will be the accomplishment of our part in the perpetuation of Service . . ." Already justified as an approach to total knowledge, the poetic exercise could be the elevation of all of creation toward God. Thus will the problem be resolved that torments Claudel and will the feeling of the altogether "earthly" vanity of that thing, poetry, be rejected.

This "logical conduct" is thus not for the poet without reversals nor personal dramas; on the contrary, it is the fruit of a dramatic tension toward justification. (Would not to know things, for example, in all justice, be to allow oneself to be invaded, in the silence of mystical ecstasy, by Unity? And Parlance, in aid of what?)

When Claudel writes his great poems, at the moment at which he allows himself to be carried away by the dominating flow of the voice that transpires in him, never disengages from his double, a "conscience" that strives to justify this very act of writing. Interminably, he must bring back to the light of day this assuredly precarious truth: that speaking is the highest function attributable to a being to carry out. Thus, each time does he confront the problem of the poetic à-propos from the definition of the poem by the poem itself. First, that the design of the poet is not to move us nor to force our admiration.

> "*And the poet replies:* I am no poet,
> And I have no desire to make you laugh or cry, nor for you to love or not love my parlance . . ."

Claudel multiplies the explanations on the true nature of the poem. It is a tool, an action toward the Eternal, a thing in itself that exists by itself:

> "Thus a poem is nary like a bag of words, it is not merely
> These things that it signifies, but it is itself a sign, an
> imaginary act, creating
> The time necessary for its resolution."

Its function is to take reality from the ground (to distract nothing from it) and to elevate it to God. It arouses the participation of every detail created by Creation, the aspiration of the whole of Creation to its Creator. The poem is an *expedition* in the world, an *exploration* in the total sense of this term.

> "What people have done around me with the canon that opens the old Empires
> With the collapsible canoe that goes up the Aruwhimi with the polar expedition making magnetic observations . . .
> I will do with a poem that will no longer be Ulysses's adventure among the Lestrygons and Cyclopes, but the knowledge of the Earth,
> Man's great poem at last beyond secondary causes reconciled with eternal forces."

At last? We have yet to feel that poetry, already justified as knowledge then as testimony (participation in the known) toward God, is also *doing* par excellence, the Act.

Yet at the beginning of everything was the Verb, which made itself flesh. And before all reality was the "primordial shiver", that which has no reality but without which no reality could be born, known: motion. Just as the Eternal Verb created all things by calling them by their name, motion has as its end the creative verb. It is by the verb, which finds its origins in Motion, that all things are given to men. By arousing all things, calling all things to the knowledge of man, at the same time as it recognizes all things in man, the verb carries all things by man toward the adoration and the celebration of God. "All motion thus finally arrives at the articulation of the Name, to conceive and to name the Eternal." In this, the verb is the act par excellence. In that it embraces the world in its totality. It alone implicates, orders all things, each in its place, from the most humble to the most sublime.

> "And I who do terrible things with my voice, make that I be wholly
> This voice, a totally intelligible word . . ."

> "I am not whole if I am not whole with this world around me. It is I alone that you want! It is the whole world that you want from me!"

> "And me, it is the whole world that I must lead to its end with a hecatomb of parlance."

There is no contradiction in the poet's answer to the solicitation of *la Muse qui est la Grâce*: he rejects mystical garb (where silence's jouissance is honed) to perfect his poet's œuvre, on earth and in participation with creation:

> "Go! you will not strip the cold taste of the earth from me,
>
> This obstinacy with the earth that is in the marrow of my bones and the stone of my substance is in the black knot of my viscera!
>
> In vain! you won't consume me!
>
> In vain! the more you call me with this presence of fire and the more I withdraw down toward the solid ground,
>
> Like a great tree that goes in search of the rock and tuff of the embrace and of the screw of its forty-two roots!
>
> Whoever has bitten of the earth keeps its taste in his teeth."

Poetic parlance celebrates all earthly things in the glory of the Creator: such is Paul Claudel's highest Reason. Such, the justification he grants himself, through so many paraphrases of Scripture. From this drama played out between vocation and faith, there remains the pathetic struggle of a sensibility – toward the pulp and flesh of this world; and one of the heaviest poetic efforts there be – toward the supreme logic of intention.)

A language that grants itself gradual authority as time goes by. A will to "totality". Earthly attachment, stubbornness. Yet the limits of these conquests must nonetheless be circumscribed, in the universal drama in which relation is played out. The "Catholic" as (formal and ideal) universal ceases little by little to seem probable. The Catholic religion itself struggles to recognize the Diverse. It relativizes, ecumenicizes, translates itself. It is possible that Claudel would have rejected with full force the current movement of his Church: that movement would have deprived him of the first necessity of his poetics. In the complementarity of everything before God, happy difference is, in effect, appreciably abolished. This complementarity goes without relational drama toward the Other: without attractions, shocks or repulsion; yet it is from drama that the earthly vocation of totality is born. The One perfects itself as an (optative) unity but destroys itself in diversity (of nature and intention) in the Claudelian relation to God. There is "a total manner for not being what is". If we now assume man's diversity in nature it will have to be admitted in man's relation to God. There would be no end to the contradictory establishment of manners "for not being what is." Claudel's poetics implicitly rejects this form of diversity. His poetry thus carries the secret mark of violence: it imposes (the One). The Universal is indeed meant to be consubstantial, but substance steals away to favor the aspiration of Being. Creation includes difference, but as a variety of its totality, not as a modality of the being who, with this difference, opposes and proposes himself. For "what is not" cannot be different in its nature from "what is not." Only the Being is similar and different. The passionate search for the *Nature* of the other dissipates in the certainty of the natural complementarity of the other to the self in God. Assuredly, Claudel did not seek to become Chinese: he would have affirmed that in a way he already was. Vocation, yes. But through which difference is erased, eroded or subtilized. Claudel's poetics, open to the world, remains a tributary of the world-as-identity. Nonetheless its rigor, the ferocity of this method by which, at the level of its vocation, he was able to knead what is given, elect him to the highest level of the most ardent deporters of language. If it happens that his intention does indeed rage tyrannically, it remains that it thus fertilizes a language by which poetry (more assuredly than with a well-measured leap) continues. Because he granted (in verse) metric inspiration to human respiration, because he fills the poem with the massive shadow of the real, Claudel opens the avenues. In his vow, his option, in the abruptness of his poetics, by the dry justness of his parlance, he dominates. The ambiguity of this verb is appropriate to his nature.

He writes the supreme letter of the immobile Occident and the first song of the shared Occident.

He invokes, he represents. What? The growth, the adventure, the departure of those mystics and ravagers, who astonished the world, established themselves elsewhere, founded *another race.*

Immobile? Because that errance of its race (the regret that errance had dried up to such a degree) convinces him to have to remain, when atavism, tremors, vocation would carry him off eternally. Immobile, because of that appetite for stable œuvres that haunts Adventurers. Immobile because he is concerned with the values that perhaps mutely detach themselves from him, and the permanence and perennity of which he psalmodies with solemn rigor. Because he cries out always returning to the West, he who left three centuries ago for the West.

And why shared, other than for having, despite what he says, grafted in himself the fertile swarming, blissfulness (the opulence, the thronging) of what is born again? Shared, his expansive call, his immoderate spaces, his ascension from lands to lands. Shared, the impact of the world.

Those who demarcated the world and made it their colony. And this one testifies to the equivocation of the adventure: Saint-John Perse, the most essential poet.

A race of "fabulous eyelids", it filters and fixes the world: it is the race of clairvoyants. A people of dreamers, peopled with one same dream "striped with violence, ruse and brilliance . . .". A meagre people, of departure. *Pamphletary princes*, ascetics, who envy the portly stability of sedentaries. *Honored voyager* whose honor is of the voyage. The poet admits to his tribe: "Predators, indeed! we were." And he admits to his wandering: "The great sovereign step of the soul without a lair." But how this people (before which I in turn remain immobile, not drunken with errance, a prey to errance, feverish for rootedness) is already there suddenly, at the poet's wish, uprooted people! "We pass, and engendered by none, how well do we know the species through which we move?" The wish of the world will carry these off *far from themselves*. And I, so far from myself, do I not wander also? I wander. Yet one land alone cries for me, one house alone. Torn away, I too, for whom the poet might have sung: "We had no knowledge of legacy, nor would we know how to bequeath." And is it not from the depths of that Creole language that he drew the expression by which he marked for the first time the remove in which he maintains himself and the race in which he *dwells*: "As for me, I have removed my feet"? But the wrenching doesn't move me.

Thus have I often dreamed before the entryway to a road of earth encased in Casuarinas, and as though predestined to some calm chasm: this is perhaps the poet's House. Hidden there. But when I imagine him in his childhoods so far from mine (I who am one of those "unsonorous faces, the color of papaya and boredom . . ."), now he has already left his house. "And the house charged with honors and the year yellow between the leaves / Are but little at the heart of the man who dreams of them: / All the roads of the world eat from our hands." One aspires to enter into his house, and is surprised to hear the poet say: "And the house! The House? . . . We just left!" Preceding André Breton's, "flanking the abyss", here then the ephemeral house of Perse "that moves, with an abyssal foundation, on its anchorage . . ." These anchors that he will haul off. No doubt during that halt of his errance (my plight of no return) did he demarcate everything: the brilliance, the solitude, the *punch the color of pus*, the castor bean, the Campeachy wood, the noise, the kakos, the faint trembling of the delirious earth, the casks of sugar and *herbe-à-madame-Lalie* – but through this real a *childhood vagabondage* vents. Everything here is caught in the snare of memory. Immediately this is no *present* for me; I divine, for the errant, the need first to recuperate: the grave minutia of the one who intends to forget nothing at the place of his encampment. *Was it but that?* Yes. The mud of the mornes claws at his boots, but his gaze is distant. Yet I live in a Unique Season, and here is one who dreams: "Summer more vast than the Empire suspends from tables of space several stories of climates." The dream of leaving isn't mine.

A people full of motion. What is his silt? Not of dry earth: the earth is here, invites, flees over there; the earth is a sea. There is the "Ocean of lands" to go to.

"And the earth makes its sea noise in the distance on the corals."

"It's the earth, from all directions, weaving its tawny wool like sea byssus."

"The moving earth in its age and its very high lineage . . . and on its staggered sheets like estuary bars and breaking seas, the incessant advancement of its clay lip."

*The earth gives of its salt*. It doesn't moor the being, it carries him off, leads him. And the latter will not anchor his area to the hard soil, nor to the silt, nor to the fertile mud. Ship's Prow or High Plateau of Dreams for him. From there, one dominates and predicts. One leaves. His real silt is in his condition as passerby, and everything that carries off like the sea: horse or dromedary, cardinal wind, felt tent, river: "Not for us has the old hydra of nights dried its blood before the fire of the cities."

He cannot *establish* himself ("High though the site may be, another sea rises in the distance, and follows us."), at least he will put his glory into *assembling*. As though "caught in the high seas", he *presents* memory. He has coursed through the spaces of the world. Universal vocation, for the errant who traces the universe: "We assemble, from on high, all of this great earthly fact."

The Being of this race is the being of voyage; because the landscape and the present are *mobile* in it. Before his thin face and his feverish desire, interminably must he watch the shiver or rush of *Cybele's grenadine, the blue rollers of Africa, the cavaliers of Asia.*

(I am trying to order my "presences", I don't press them to the fixity of parlance. It is parlance, on the contrary, deaf and ingrate, that disentangles itself from the present, scurries there, to fail or to live. The solemn voyage, its solemn relation is totalization. I see the Book in it: Bestiaries, Portolanos, High Registers of Knowledge. I seek the relation there in vain, hard and heavy to endure. Poet of essence, and the last chronicler: who, against and astride the horrible cracking of the earth, dares, in absolute, a new "currency" of the world."

To watch the world roll, drunken boat, and keep its logbook, – from there, by force, like a vocation of nothingness (of the unrooted) or of disturbance (of the unfixed), like an appetite for transcendence that will find satisfaction in no œuvre, like a delectation of Being, led step by step to the only dwelling that it will elect, eternal and stable – comes parlance. "I will take up my course to the Numides, along the inalienable sea." Where to, if not "a great poem born of nothing", "a great delible poem", and which way? – "Numerous are the ways, and our dwellings uncertain. . . ." Here is the universal world: conductor of the lay. Let it be said: here the universe exists so that the poem may be.

The poet thus becomes combined with the voyager: his only shelter is the poem. Against the principial *disturbance*, the assurance of the verb. Having no place, the seer founds exile. He claims it, provokes it if necessary. "I will inhabit my name". The exile of Crusoe in the city, the exile of the officer who secretly elects himself officiant. For *exile did not arise yesterday*: it began with the departure of the first caravel. It is not a state, but a passion. *Further yet than the rolling storm*, he is in the voyage, he is also at a halt. See how he assaults the being with perfidity, disturbs him anew. For in the poem entitled *Exil*, it is said: "Here I am restituted to my native shore . . ." Is it exile from Europe, or from America? Why this disturbance? Whence, departure? For real, exile is exigency. Leaving it, this poet will not enter into a house (if not an ephemeral one yet, raised against a headland, a high pavilion), but in that ultimate dwelling where "the obscure birth of language" stirs.

Parlance is place, and poetry all together "road of exile and alliance". The One, diverted from the world, struggles in the echo of his name.

("Alliance": what is stable. But also, at last: — relation?)

Language of "creation", true force. For the wanderer, here is the "supreme altercation of man at the heights of being, parlance!" The altercation: the remove of those who know. If the poem is delible, it is because in the world it has only itself for a reference. It avows the nothingness from which it proceeds, but never throws itself into question. The "Currency" did not have as its end the signification of different flavors, but the unification of the dispersed leap. For which the universal motion can mingle in the end with rhetorical fecundity. So does Saint-John Perse recognize through Dante who was the epic voice of his true dwelling: the Occident. He makes the whole "West" into his house. What he sings here is a vocation: the "West" universalized, "where the dream is action, and action innovative." Here then is the unfurling – since parlance and dwelling coincide at last – of the great generalizing inspirations by which errance is assumed (illuminated): "It is the whole entire being that comes to the consecration of the poem."

But generalized magnificences cannot replace the nettle of the ravines, the stairway of the steppes, the snow of the berries. The world is irreducible to one parlance, even if it is "total". The hot porosities of *Éloges*, the stratified opacities of *Anabase*, the liquid space of *Exil* prevail over the totalizing rustling of the *Vents*. They are the poet's share.

They are, perhaps without his consent, what he feels he has preserved in irreducible *people*, in the very place where his project consisted in magnification toward the One. In order for parlance to be the place, he would in effect have needed for it to root in real silt. The vocation of the Occident, that is indeed uncertain silt. For, did the Occident in turn consent to this higher and haughty function that Saint-John Perse imagines for it? For the voyager, "return from the hot countries", nothing is less certain. The action has limits, unity fractures. Man, vexed, cries "the poet's scandal", which is indeed the "bitter censor of a vindictive soul" *par excellence*. The errant he remains will not build the new House by the Shore. The exigency for exile does not abdicate being; it must always take to the sea. The poet, in the margins of his world recreates a world. "From the steps of exile, he manages a solitude more populated than any empire's land." He banishes from the world the City that betrays his vow. It is the mark of Transhumants; like the fistful of dirt they throw defiantly ahead of their steps, before bringing down their column.

To this double observation (parlance rustling with its abstract want, the "Latin eldership", more threatened, more fleeting, more illegitimate than ever), the Navigator feels the dense resistance of the universe: the poem *only is* because the universes oppose its opacities, join them there. What was endlessly Memory (what the errant only sang at the moment of separation – granting himself life from seeing it — : the strange evening primrose, the familiar Banyan tree, the too naked mangrove tree), that is what is *left*. The infinite presence of the other. Yet, having left these tracts of memory, this limited present, also uninhabitable ("and what is all this that is not passion, and that hasn't the taste of eternity?"), the poet projects – this is his recourse – into the future. The universal will be postulated, for not being able to be experienced. The distance was marked yesterday by errance and exile; it is now marked by the pilgrimage toward tomorrow. "And we have no rank among men of the moment." – "We are shepherds of the future." Parlance, vanquished here, and which is not the place of constancy, is born again from its defeat; the poet resuscitates his vow: "To breathe with the world remains his proper and mediating function."

On the evening of the fertile Voyage, and after the impossible rhetorical dream, the future in which the universal will be articulated (but no longer the magnified, totalizing universal) is yet praised in the passion of *going*. "Like the nomadic Conquerors masters of an infinite space, the great transhumant poets, honored by their shadow, escape at length the illuminations of the ossuary. Wrenching themselves from the past, they watch the incessant growth before them of the race on a track that proceeds from them . . ."

From them? Indeed; from that passion for exile. Of that race that took place in its errance and limited the world, saw it and wanted to fix it. The poet of the "antique" race and that "nameless" face is that Discoverer of lands, that man who surveys, raising his "darkened" heart, "where avidity was, and what was ardent, and so much unrevealed love . . ." Here the voyage *includes* conquest; the poet's vow transcends and absolves the bloodiness of errance.

Necessary poetry. From the glorious praise of lands to the assumption of the universal West to the promise of shared futures, it *follows the course of the world*. If the assumption is recognized to be illegitimate in its sole sumptuousness, if the future is not to be called out (for what it fathoms there of faults and wounds), if the Chronicle of Conquerors inconveniences us, even if Praise has attempted to raise a being-of-the-world at the expense of the being (the latter is happily preserved by the very act of praising), yes, a ritual memory rather than an ungrateful and implicated present, — what parlance has yet more densely figured in the drama in which the solitary Occident suddenly surprised itself in the face of the clay recesses of the world, and veiled before them its proud, stirred and threatened face?

# On the impossible in poetry

Predictable defeat of the generous who intended to allocate himself "essentially" to the other; totalitarian constraint of the Catholic for whom the other is mingled in the commuted essence of the Whole; flight and overview, distance nourished with succulences, by which the shared being is nonetheless separated from the dramatic melee. Marginal poetics of the world, which *exposed* the world. From none of these will plenitude be drawn. They are exemplary: but this example does not consecrate. *Implicate*, yes.

The threatened being who ventures and plays in the drama of the world, that is our being. How impossible is the vow of totality! Necessary, and illusory. It intends to force man (the poet) to watch with lucidity, attentiveness, selectiveness, *over all fronts at once*. Without forgetting that all idealism erupts without fail by every breach. The vow of the earth is not the earth; "contact" is often a lure, whose fruitful consequences might easily be foreclosed to fall for the absolute desperation of its fascination. Here again, to embody the relative.

From the One to the universe, if it happens, the relation (the road) winds, discomfited or uncertain, at the non-global, non-absolute practices sewn through space, from the Diverse to the Common. The absolute (as it always does) will gather farther along.

# FROM THE DIVERSE TO THE COMMON

Thus the motion toward Elsewhere that punctuates French literature with works that are admittedly less and less exotic. Occidental letters have experienced the progression, from relations of discovery, from first narratives (through the dead time of adventure stories, so foreign to the settings in which they were situated) to contemporary ethnographic studies, marked with a new respect for world civilizations. In turn, literary works found themselves renewed, reinstated.

Some Europeans cover these two domains: writers and ethnographers by vocation, they seem to have drawn new nourishment from the teachings of their discipline, enough to enrich what I would still call the "search for the self": and they profited from their writerly vocation, from their obligation to be sincere and rigid toward themselves, to return its true meaning to the exercise of this activity devoted more than any other to the "search for the Other". These men propose that we attend to works that are by turn *milestone-books* (in the experience and orientation of occidental sensibility) and *relay-books* (with a total, unprejudiced approach to extra-occidental civilizations).

If these preoccupations are commonly shared, they are very literally inscribed in Michel Leiris's project. He carried to extreme limits the state of exorbitance, the experience of modern chaos, with poems from the beginning of *Haut Mal* and with *Aurora*. But already, among the raging explosions of these poems, several questions regarding language are inscribed: we see that the author protests all at once against "the rational galley-slaves and striped syntaxes", "the profound tyranny of words and tattoos of chance". And already, in this transfigured Voyage that is *Aurora*, "the horror before any sort of fixation", but also the search for an Elsewhere too abstract to procure anything other than a saturation of chaos. Here is how the "voyage" ends: by a very humble return. "I stopped near the pont Notre-Dame, on a winter's day. My body numb, made heavy by the cold, immobilized itself against one of the great metallic rings hanging over the river bank . . ." The poet already sensed that Elsewhere is complicit with Here, and that at the point of his departure there were the same enigmas (same intensity) to resolve. The last lines of the book attest to this: "Further from me, fairly high to the right, my vitrified gaze was hooked to the tip of Notre-Dame's rise, a temple that was neither built by Semiramis nor by the Queen of Saba, but on stones on which it is said that the principle secrets of Nicolas Flamel are engraved, more enigmatic even than those of Paracelsus." It is no less true that, if the "search for the self" begins for Michel Leiris with excesses of the self, if it leads to the exercise of its chaos, and if he is wary of the hopes or sciences of the Nomad, he made a summary attempt to elucidate a primary "norm" – that of language – and undertook a first "means", that of the Voyage and of the experience of the Other. He will inscribe these attempts in the real: attaching himself to his more and more profound childhood and adult experiences (from which he will build his literary universe), studying in the world the places and beings which will strengthen him in the knowledge, always approached but never attained, of human becoming (he will be an ethnographer). And he will develop into exigency what was but an instinctual reaction, organize into themes what was but a cry, study in the real-other what had haunted him in the other-imaginary. In solidarity he will attempt a search for the self and a quest for humanities, a project and a science.

The experience of "deregulation" distances Michel Leiris from literary activity: unavowed desire for the "*Règle du Jeu*". He is bored. Led also to leave, to "make himself other", by the discovery of jazz and the shock of black sculpture. The chance of reinvigoration, the revelation of an art whose unfetterings are necessary, fecund justification of chaos, invitation to go out of bounds. He is conquered by the opposite of himself, by that communicable immoderation whose laws are as strict as they are profound. Soon Leiris will leave, ahead of *L'Afrique fantôme*.

A milestone-book. The author only left in order to find himself again. He did not go to meet the Other but went ahead of his own ghost, the ghost of Michel Leiris. Instead he finds the ghost of the other. A book that testifies to  a certain disorientation, purveyor of good will, that effectively portrays an era and a style of approach to the world. The individual, hounding himself, sceptical, suddenly moved, most often worried about his reactions, conveying his dreams and nightmares with care, to the point where his dreams, which relate to his past, take up almost as much space as what he sees of Africa. (One imagines that during such voyages, through this sort of rehashing of his past, Michel Leiris inaugurated the technique that orchestrated *Biffures* and *Fourbis*, his great literary ensembles.) The beauties of the work, the tone of sincere intransigence, lead us to loosen its lines of force. Scepticism: "Saw no elephants, naturally"; total freedom vis-à-vis the setting: "Moonlight that is altogether unhealthy as well as splendid, with shady clouds covering the star and a very long stretch of lit swamp over the sea"; disappointment, often: "The voyage only changes us sometimes. Most of the time you remain sadly as you always were." First projected titles: *L'ombre de l'aventure, Le promeneur du Cancer*; disillusion, deaf literature. Here it is not a matter of ethnography, despite the relating of sacrifices toward the end of the book. In other words, the author has not yet accepted his vocation, developed his scientific activity. The writing is made of notes or notations, it is a series of ruptures, we are far from that *fugal method* (the expression is Jean Laude's, from a conversation with Michel Leiris) which will constitute the writer's style. The accomplishment of this style will accompany the man's awareness; and by exercising his occupation, Leiris will be led to reconnect fully with the literature that had wearied him.

Ethnography is indeed not literature. On first consideration, that human science is not without requiring a certain share of inhumanity. In addition, for ethnographers, the practice of their science is always accompanied by a reflection on its foundations. They prop up a sort of humanism that, more or less imprecise, more or less active, keeps them from the multiple dangers that threaten observation: incomprehension, prejudices, enthusiasms, the obscure feeling of superiority of the observer. Be that as it may, observations, relations, monographs, analyses, form the basis for ethnography and must not be intermixed with the "literary".

Leiris grapples, at the beginnings, with these difficulties. Too honest to want to escape the exigencies of his occupation, he nonetheless feels unavowed discomfort toward it, when he draws up "reports". He develops a tendency toward irony that might be said to be his manner of "distancing". "Relatively long struggle. The bull is knocked onto his left side. But it is not the good side; he must be turned onto his right side. So the bull disentangles from his bonds. He must be restrained again. At last, he is knocked onto his right side. It comes close to turning into a corrida . . ." Similarly, he never sacrifices the real for the solemn: "The bull, slow to die, grumbles while his trachea is butchered." From the outset, as though by instinct, Leiris resists a certain number of conventions of the ethnographic genre: he will swing from the necessary and partial examination of "primitive" civilizations to the complex study of relations between civilizations such as they are currently practised in various regions of the world. Within the objective limits he imposes on himself, the ethnographer is concerned with not veiling truths he judges to be inevitable. That the adaptation of peoples to the conditions of the modern world could only be the concern of those peoples themselves; that the historical movement leads all peoples (but through how many mortal pitfalls?) toward a universal fraternity of various civilizations. Ethnography is thus placed under the influence of a becoming, and no longer anchored to the limitations of a past that was informative without sanctioning excesses. These truths are germinating, if only at the level of reluctance, in the first works of Leiris. Soon, (awakened from *L'Afrique fantôme*), his notations will give way to writing, the impetus to theme, "thoughts" to thought, rupture to continuity. It is not surprising that he inaugurated his texts on ethnography itself with the critical preface to *L'Afrique fantôme*, which introduces the 1950 edition.

There, he inventories every error, examines every proposition, redresses every work perspective:

Condemnation of exoticism: ("fallacious attempt to make oneself other").

Critique of the "climate" of *L'Afrique fantôme*: "the human problems that . . . were already presenting themselves only struck me when they were cloaked in the aspect of absolutely glaring abuse, without, however, wrenching me from my dreamer's subjectivism."

Explanation of the intention masked by the book: "Passing from an almost exclusively literary activity to the practice of ethnography, I intend to break with the intellectual habits that were hitherto mine and, in contact with men from a culture other than mine, and of another race, and to collapse the partitions between which I was suffocating and enlarge my horizon to a truly human measure."

Position with regard to ethnography "thus envisioned": "(It) . . . could only disappoint me: a human science remains a science and detached observation could not alone beget *contact*."

Solution advocated by this preface: " . . . that there is no ethnography or exoticism that can be sustained in the gravity of the questions asked, on a social level, by the disposition of the modern world and that, if contact between men born in very different climes is not a myth, it is in the exact measure by which it can be realized by the common work against those, in the capitalist society of our twentieth century, who are the representatives of the slavery of old."

Leiris's effort will consist henceforth in leaning ethnographic practice in the direction of this study of real contacts; in this perspective he reconciles the search for the self with the search for the other, placing them in solidarity after having ceased to intermix them. He will accomplish in the real the once de-formed dialectic (in the imaginary) of his first books. Two visits to the Antilles will confirm his intention to examine contacts and civilizations there.

These countries offer a privileged example of cultural symbiosis. Leiris will be convinced by this complexity that tends toward harmony and evolves, one might say, before the eyes of the observer. All ethnography of the Antilles ceases to be strictly recapitulative, engages the future in the present, forces a consideration of collisions between cultures, and (despite the racism that holds sway in these countries) confirms that it is not utopic to conceive of the advent one day of a truly composite civilization.

*Contacts de civilisations en Martinique et en Guadeloupe* : "objective" humanism for which we indicated that ethnography had such an urgent need, the necessity to move beyond observation and tend toward broader intentions, here then, at the very level of observation, integrated to it and without the observer being able to neglect them, do they impose themselves: precisely because observation is concerned with contacts, syntheses, cultural collisions and harmonies. This is the meaning of the attention Leiris granted to the Antilles: they illustrate his intention; he confronts a complexity, a synthesis, a becoming in action. Discomfort, "distanciation", can be succeeded by solidarity. Only then, reconciled with ethnography, does he grant it at last the right to serenity, for its having resolved some of its internal contradictions.

An Antillean engaged with the national problematic who will surface sooner or later in this country might reproach this book for insufficiently defining constants. But it is not for Michel Leiris to do the work of the Antillean, nor to disengage them from the depths of alienation. Just as he slowly ordered his themes until he conceived *La Règle du Jeu*, he was also able to give a body of thought to his practice of ethnography. And just as the writing of his last literary works is developed in swaths of prose, motives that continually relay one another, attempting more and more to define a complexity of being ("man's condition"), thus, faced with the complexity of a country, does he employ a style of approach that neglects absolutely nothing of analytical detail and is no less appropriate to a general view. Meticulous, tormented, illuminated writing. A complex and dense book about a complex and dense situation. Interlacing information out of which a presence wells.

Search for the self: a writer who in his language and in his intention asserts himself; search for the other: a scholarly man who conquers lines of force, the bases for his discipline. What might be called Michel Leiris's humanism is born of that double effort of solidarity toward the world of others and a common future.


(And it is convincing that ethnography as an activity continues imperceptibly here and there: as a technique of social analysis, as a methodology of action, as a sub-work of works, as a problematic of communication. (Putting aside cases in which it is a crude pretext for police investigation or political espionage). We hate ethnography: whenever, executing itself elsewhere, it does not fertilize the dramatic vow of relation. The distrust we feel toward it comes not from the displeasure at being watched, but from the resentment at not watching in turn. And not for its weaning us from the satisfaction of equivalence, but for its obfuscation and ransacking (at least as it is practiced) of the richness of all relations, of this relationship: the world at last alive, suffered, shared. "The attentive observer" that is (or was) the ethnographer must *inscribe himself in the drama of the world*: beyond his analysis – in principle, "solitary" – he must live a poetics (sharing). Thus Leiris.)

The exotic word effectively anticipated these two worlds, the first of which (that of the author) goes in some ways to meet the second, which is the unknown. To begin with, exotic literature proposes the charitable, regenerative feeling of a rupture between two modes of the real. Discovery, whether strange, provoked, or imposed, requires accommodations that confirm being in its truth or, on the contrary, senses it outside of itself. This genre of literature demands amazement, the unexpected, or, conversely, withholding, systematic refusal, or attention, study – in sum the relation between a new force and an established force. The œuvre of Alejo Carpentier contradicts the principles of genre; for if it is possible to qualify it as exotic in the eyes of the European reader, in the way he is displaced through an unfamiliar new World, it nonetheless attests to an original situation: a man who participates intimately in both worlds, one of which he will at last have to decide is Foundation.

Born in Havana to a European father and a Cuban mother, Carpentier spends his young manhood in Paris, after which he returns to the Antilles and the Latin America of his childhood. Henceforth he moves, not from discovery to discovery, but from marker to marker. He finds in himself that which the landscape proposes. He tends, not toward an accommodation, but deeply, toward a synthesis. The problems he discusses do not implicate an integration – whether or not possible – to a strange world, but the necessary conciliation between two secreted "orders". If this conciliation passes through judgments, if, for example, Carpentier examines occidental culture with severity, don't assume a bias, but the imperious necessity for him to confront his various values stripped bare. Here is the Occident, stripped of the taboos with which it arrayed itself in order to perpetuate its domination; here is a new world, with its excesses, its aspirations, its values. The œuvre presents a (non-exotic) character of debate; the novel is elucidation. But this œuvre also opens onto an experience shared by millions of men; for it is a debate of culture-shocks, and what is played out here is the possible avenue of a unity, a lifestyle.

*Le Partage des eaux* is the book of a reconquest. Under the pretext of an official mission (the search for a primitive musical instrument), the hero, a South American, deracinated man, prisoner of the facticity of a New York of pseudo-intellectuals, flees an environment that has become suffocating for him: the life he leads in the big city gnaws at and tortures him. But it is difficult to wrench oneself from the drama of daily wear and tear. The immersion back into "primitive" realms (the virgin lands of the High Orinoco incidentally) will be heralded by prevarications, returns, dramatic interrogations. It will be necessary to leave the modernity that marks and invades, in order to reach the spaces in which each becomes "master of his own time". Yes, as he penetrates the distant lands, our musician seems to follow the course of time backwards, from age to age: he leaves behind the South American capital with its romantic operas, the lands of the Horse, the less maintained lands of the Dog, and from retreat to retreat arrives, after many challenges that figure the stages of an initiation (storms, shipwrecks on the Orinoco, terrifying virgin forest) to the "Valley of Suspended Time" that can thus be said to be the valley of the first age. Yet there is already some ambiguity: finding himself henceforth in the essential landscape of his childhoods, he will be torn from it by an airplane gone in search of him; the modern world doesn't let go of its prey. And when the voyager, leaving his wife once more, as well as an insipid mistress dismantled by the first expedition, will want at last to find the road of origins, he will come up against impassable obstacles; this voyage is not to be started over. One must become resigned to the flight of ages, accept one's era, attempt at last to reconcile the virtues of that America (encountered again on the incline leading to the search of lost time) and the powers of the modern world. Failed attempt: "The truth, the smothering truth, now I understand, is that the people from those distant regions never believed in me. I was an assumed being. Rosario herself must have seen me as a Visitor, incapable of remaining indefinitely in the Valley of Suspended Time. I remember the strange look she gave me when she saw me writing feverishly, for days on end, in a place where writing responded to no necessity." But consciousness as well: and of a possible *re-union*. For in this did the failure swell: that the hero of *Partage* is, come what may, a man of art, of knowledge; a man sensitive to the presence of History, who was unable to fully live what he experienced at the edge of the dateless river, even though he consented to it for life. At least he will not have returned disarmed, no longer will he be the puppet of the ramshackle city, dissolving little by little. Having seen the Eldorado, experienced the vanity of flights, one senses at the end that he will attempt that synthesis of which we speak, that he will "undertake" that language.

Must one live, must one express oneself? To live, to possess one's truth. To express, to know at last that one belongs to one's time. And not one without the other: that is the lesson of the *Partage des eaux*.

Do those two imperatives correspond to the two cultural groups that oppose one another (to meet again) in Carpentier's œuvre? The first, which constitutes the very flesh of this œuvre, and is the nature and reality of the "other America" – and the second, the machine of the Occident, which marked time by the implacable clock of History. Until today, by the monologue imposed on these new lands, expression has been the prerogative of the Occident; Carpentier's effort aims to give an expression, a consciousness, a form, a time, to that timeless truth, hidden, barely lived, which is that of his "zone". Such is the difficult synthesis. We will see what its modalities might be, or whether some impassable obstacle, like a second voyage of the hero of the Orinoco, will resist its accomplishment.

The Antilles, South America: it's the same recourse to the past (that we learn to know at last), same tension toward a future, same search for unity (inscribed in the elements of the real but whose dynamic is delayed by all sorts of obstacles); it is the attachment to the earth, the unprotesting character of existence, the immediacy of nature, the necessity of marrying African, European, Indian cultural elements, whose impact must be achieved undamaged: the vocation of an organic (and no longer ideal) universal.

Contributing to this work, Carpentier's œuvre is also an exploration of its various elements. *Le Royaume de ce monde* is a fresco of Haiti at the moment of its great revolutions. There intervenes a sorcerer, Mackandal, whose predictions and the surprising power attributed to him to borrow at will from all forms of animal life, nourish the black revolt with magic forces. Over the course of four revolutions, the hero of the book, Ti Noël, will be supported and led by the memory of the sorcerer until, as a powerless old man, he finally understands that memory is not enough. "At this time, returned to man's condition, the old man had a moment of supreme lucidity. In the space of a second, he experienced the most important moments of his life; he saw once more the heroes who had revealed the force and richness of his distant African ancestors, making him believe in a better future. He felt himself grow old beneath the weight of innumerable centuries." On the ruins of the society of abolished slavery and at the dawn of just as terrible an era, when old white masters are replaced with aristocrats, "fence-sitters . . . that caste of quadroons that was presently appropriating old dwellings," Ti Noël takes stock of his male condition: "He had assumed his share of hereditary tasks, and though he had reached the last degree of misery, he, in turn, left that heritage intact. His flesh had done its time." The old order of things is exorcized, and their very elements take part in a symbolic purification: "And while the slit-throated bulls bawled at the summit of Bonnet de l'Évêque, the armchair, the screen, the volumes of *l'Encyclopédie*, the music box, the doll, the moonfish all suddenly flew away in the collapse of the last ruins of the old dwelling. All the trees laid down, their tops facing south, uprooted. All night a sea-water rain fell on the mountain's flanks, leaving traces of salt." Thus throughout the book did we come to know the clandestine motives for the black momentum of Haiti: loyalty to the Ancestors, vaudun. Insufficient resources against the movement of history. Once again, the terms of the enormous contract governing these lands are laid out: unknown power, timeless truth, not acute in the consciousness, and on the other hand the inevitable historical process, that much obliged *modernity*.

The search for origins, the elucidation of myths, the ambition of a language that is as customary as it is literary: here Alejo Carpentier's preoccupations are imperious. We measure the difficulties of the enterprise: that there is an opposition between the existence of the Indian woman, Rosario, and that of the hero of *Partage*, be-tween the sorcery of Mackandal and the conscious struggle between the modern architectures of the tropical cities and the growths of Nature whose roots split the thickest of walls, between the wonder, the magic, the timelessness of that America in painful gestation, and the exigencies of modern times. But it is in the knowledge of these irreconcilabilities that their synthesis, their future, is made possible; Mackandal is a powerful hero in my heart, and I struggle to loosen his solitude from the frozen fields of historical silence; Carpentier's book all of a sudden takes on positive meaning.

"Here, in reality, it was not the inbred peoples who had un-leashed themselves, like those that history had kneaded at the cross-roads of Ulysses's sea, but the great races of the world, more distant, more different, those who, for millennia, had mutually ignored one another on the planet." "I asked myself whether the role those coun-tries played in the history of men wasn't to make possible, for the first time, certain cultural symbioses."

In other words, synthesis is foremost a vocation for synthesis. Let us, Antilleans, not withdraw from the knowledge of and the claim to black virtues and traditions, as well as those, Indian and European, which made their way to us; but let us hesitate before adjusting them. May this hot rediscovery of the self not incline us to a sterile and exclusive imploring of the past. This vocation is projec-tive: the shock of cultures is a dynamic passion for cultures.


By turns language beats a black rhythm, runs in the breadth of Spanish prose. The trail alerts Antillean storytellers, and the newest picaresque irony. A realism inherited from the Occident (a revolu-tion, a Haitian street at the time of prosperous slavery, a staging at the Havana opera) follows without discontinuity a semi-ritual chant (at the moment, for example, of the great spectacles and disarrays of the jungle): the novel illustrates its intention. Here we are at the crossroads of Cultures, at another parting of the waters, before a new measure for knowledge and for life.

Here at last, a project whose double movement we will observe: wishing oneself earth and tree to gain one's liberty; free to identify with the earth and the tree. Poetry is a convulsive search toward "a shadow of the self that in itself gives signs of friendship." And if this other, internal, is *he who knows*, his approach is nonetheless difficult and dark; it is only achieved in the self in stages, whether wrenching or euphoric, according to the vagaries of faltering. The particularity of the black writer has rested in this: that he was first conscious of that which, between he and this other self, was maintained by the force of barriers.

While one understands the importance of such will to freedom, one can be less open to that other necessity, a sort of liberation of the fundamental being. One will contest the value of the plunge back into obscure forces, will deny that here there is a necessity for postulate identification with the earth and the tree; one will impose, at the very level of poetics, an absolute clarity of *reasons* – in short, one will be indignant at abandon and demand reserve. But abandon to forces was justified, and reserve exerted: thus is a perfection discernible in the first works of Césaire.

In the language of our time, the *Cahier d'un retour au pays natal* is a "moment": the flamboyant overturning of a consciousness, the elevation toward all of the new will of some. It is also a cry: plunged into the black wisps of the earth. It is an organization: the poem follows a course that is not sacrificed to the ardor of telling and which does not tyrannize speech. To arrive at full self-awareness, the man begins here by discovering his country; land of flourish, of bonhomie and miseries, in its pettiness as in the brilliancy of its sun.

And traversing his country, carried by "the lapidary jouissance of the torrents", tightening his fists before the spectacle of the lowest misery, before "the great immobile night, the stars more dead than a skewered balafon", the poet enumerates what is his, and his alone. And he claims a place in the light of the world. It is, in the fullest sense, knowledge of the world and of the self: here, Claudel's vow is verified, illuminated in and by experience. The importance of verification is in its being undertaken in a *real* birth (the all-powerful sense of being at last born to the light of the world in turn illuminates consciousness and reinforces the first claim); before, only the night of slavery had existed, then of that (imposed) non-self-knowledge. Here man is at last upright, and he sees himself in his brothers:

*truly the older brothers of the world . . .*
*flesh of the flesh of the palpitating world of the very motion of the*
*world!*

Expression arms itself with the adequation of man to his country; adequation: knowledge, foundation, ardor. Why this election of the earth? Because it is, in the birth of man, the first and perhaps the only force from which he may ask for force.

*And now suddenly force and life assail me like a bull and I renew ONAN who devoted his sperm to the fecund earth . . .*

There is justice in the idea of "communication" with the world, enclosing it. This communication founds revolt, and revolt authorizes. *Modern* valorization: man tends to gather universal, contradictory, and converging forces, populates himself with them; also does the poet assume not only his birth, and that of his people, but all knowledge, the actual vow of the human. The poem breathes the joy of the newfound world. An accomplice of the universe, mutely populated with the "secret of great communications and great combustions", the poem is fortified in order first to recover his universe. But if the discovery of the world brings with it the revival of the self and of his area, meanwhile, the newfound consciousness of country and being combined sets him forth at last on "the great stage of the world."

In *Les Armes miraculeuses* the climate, the genre, the profusion, the atmosphere of the vegetation and the appearance of the geography that characterize the country of the Antilles. Also the history of that land "prophesied as beautiful" by the poet. Finally, rhythm as expression. The *"Armes miraculeuses"* are those opposed by the poet to any attempt to denature, any strange will that might tend to despoil it of itself. There is no tormented minutia here, but the solar deployment of a *nature*; still the inventory of the poet's "reasons" is accomplished.

What, in these works, motivates excellence: that we are endlessly drawn from country to being, from poetry to knowledge, from one situation to all possible situations, from one man to total man; that these intentions, these approaches, implicate, underscore, command one another in the deepest of ways.

Further abstraction of the country, the brilliancy of *Soleil Cou Coupé*; in this book the poem abandons its direct hold, the ornament of the earth, to specify its themes. At the level of entity pitched here by the poet, fixed in its non-receiving end, lynchers, jailers, missionaries, the pastor, command him. Against "naked law" and "the Chief of Staff of crime" and "the effortless geometry of lies", it is necessary, here, in the space of the poem, to mobilize all of the self's forces,

> *the Earth at last drunk*
> *and the clear language of its thunder,*

because

> *the weakness of many men is that they neither know how to*
> *become a stone nor a tree,*

because those who denounced themselves were subjected to that weakness (for having been relegated to themselves and to others man cut them from their origins, from the world), and because at the opposite such is the force: of primary authorization. *Soleil Cou Coupé* is simple reaction and literal search for liberation values. Strained humor snickers there. Themes, schemes. Returning to the magnificence of the birth of man to his world, such that beneath cries and rendings it bursts out in *Armes*; to the labor of being, enthusiastic yet lucid, of which the *Cahier* is the instrument as well as the "report". In other words, its importance erupts in the poem of this parcel of land "fixed by our will alone": because the most generous way of being in the world is first to be born to one's own world.

Césaire's world will be the world of becoming – personal and historical. What does poetic emancipation bring? A "dilation on the scale of the world", of course, but also the profound sense of one's own situation in the world:

*It is not a matter as with the ancient lyric of the immortalization of an hour of sorrow or of joy. Here we are well beyond the anecdote, at the heart of man, in the bubbling crevice of his destiny . . . And in the one that I am the one I will be rises onto the tips of his feet . . .*

To be born to the world, is as much to come to the light of the sun as to that of consciousness – it is to be born to History (not subjected to it). Here, this man is profoundly engaged in a collective adventure. He cannot, without risking losing himself, abstract himself from his commonality. But he cannot, without the risk of denaturing himself, become enclosed in his nature. A surge beyond contradictions, a passion for integration, thirst for totality.

*Poetic knowledge is that in which man sprays the object with all of its mobilized riches.*

A poetics also of surpassing. What was historically situated, condemned to dry out, what was a moment (the famous "anti-racist racism"), Césaire killed it (exceeded it) in the person of his *Rebelle*. Such is the lesson of this tragedy: *Et les chiens se taisaient . . .* It was necessary for the hero to die, after having suffered the amazement and the weight of the birth of all (but also, after having killed his master with his own hands: that act is conceived in the tragedy as the only rite appropriate to true "birth").

"Négritude", if it is understood to be the reaction against the denounced enemy, abolishes itself as soon as a being has taken possession of himself, after the first tragedy and the first cry. Only then in the name of the totality of experience is this enemy felled. And if it is understood to be the quality of being black, it never did exist dramatically (other than through that first struggle): by understanding this quality the poet understands his universality.

If humanity draws itself, not as some sort of indivision in which everything must be brought back to *an essence*, but as the deepened relation of the same to the other, of the diverse to the alike, each will be required to be himself, integral and integrated (but not assimilated to the other) in totality. Where there is no need to renounce being oneself (being black), that is where the vow alights. Négritude is always a moment, a *total* struggle, and as a result brief and flamboyant. Everywhere blacks are oppressed, there is négritude. Each time they pick up a cutlass or a gun, négritude ceases (for them). It is vow and passion of the poet: inscribed in the story, it does not project itself into history. The struggle of those who are damaged begins with it, and carries on elsewhere: thus the relation between the complex circuit of the emancipation of peoples, of political struggle, of free communication. The dreamed quota is realized through the number of acts. Thus it is possible to continue to cry négritude without enriching it with its own possible extension: the act by which it exceeds itself. And it is even possible to misunderstand négritude, under pressure and in the pressure of a struggle, and accomplish it nonetheless, by acting in the real.

It is also that the "cultural zone" in which the poet exercises his poetics is still the over-signified poetics of the other. Which is true of all of us. We outline the Other whose Occidental *Je* has pronounced the vow: we do not disengage him. He surfaces in the struggles and sufferings of exterminated and victorious peoples. Just as there is an obliged passage from the poetic call of the emergence of the world to the collective struggle to establish oneself in the world (without confusing the call or the struggle with their techniques of course), the relation to the other also requires that the poet take on (by "willful" force and decision, when a conscious community has not yet been established – or by natural growth, when it already exists) the new "cultural zone" (even, and even more, if it is a composite) as his own. New: not so much by the nature of its components, which could only enrich themselves, evolve in their relations, enlarge concrete possibilities, precisely in the manner for taking charge of these components, ensuring the dynamic of their fecundity. The poetics of the œuvre skids over its own surface if it doesn't erupt in the open, collective, abundant fertility of an assumed culture. More than totalizing négritude, the œuvre requires totalizing rooting. One does not root oneself in vows (even those that proclaim the root) nor in a distant earth (even if it is mother-earth, Africa), because in this way, one initiates an (other) abstract, universal process, thus contributing *by one's own richness* to the total relation. One must walk from the vow to the real: in order to emancipate another vow. These works of Césaire's *will take on* their full meaning when they will be integrated to a literature of the country itself: to a concerted proposition of exchange with the Other (with all others), in which the exchange will be known to be different and convergent, free and implicated in that freedom. The œuvre risks paling, tarnishing (even when taken on elsewhere, as in France or Africa) if it does not receive its own country's approval: if the land against which it abuts remains absent: decerebrated, assimilated: not creative. The poet calls to his land, but the poem claims it. For the land is the poet's ultimate argument; but it is the secret generator of the poem. In other words: the poem can precede and found the land's "reason", but cannot live far from its substance and savor, which it signifies.

In other words: the land must have trembled at least once in its total freedom for the poem, which signifies the land, to be forever installed in its truth. The *communities* that man unendingly poeticizes (sanctions or postulates) are crudely bound to historicity.

Thus is Césaire's enterprise first best qualified as a *cri de conscience*. In the cry of liberty, man may exceed his cry. But excess is his choice, and the cry his reserve. Out of that double point of view will we see the *Cahier* and *Armes* draw a quasi organic unity of language and an unfailing poetics.

# On a deficiency of poetry

There is a calamity worse than retreat (into oneself), reflection (of the other) or abstraction (of everything): it is the unnatural, not imposed from beyond but intimately presumed. The claim (an avatar) to universality leads here and there, unnoticeably, to an imbroglio, a sterile *chassé-croisé*, in which the Occidental wants to *make himself into* that which he is not, wants to change lands, when he hasn't Ségalen's heroic lucidity (but it is not for changing lands, it is up to each to change his own land, to save it); and in which the non-Occidental wants to become and to remain everything (cultivated, open, conciliatory, knowledgeable, synthetic, humanist: "free"), when all he does is to adjourn alignment. Exceed as well the temptation for excess.

What power of imminence must the man of Occident have in order to remain himself, without forgetting himself, nor despairing, while respecting and calling the distance of the other (and in reality, each time a people escaped his power, this man spoke of his *decadence*, of his *abdication*, or else hurriedly signified that he "made the world", instead of meditating on the real *promotion* that opened him to the world through that denial); to this other, much pondered passion, to rupture *in depth*, knowing that a more certain meeting (liberated, consensual relation) is there? For now, our common poetics require these contrary approaches. *If you cease to be yourself, where will the relation be? If I make myself freely (freely?) you, what languages, in your language, or in mine, will we exchange?*

If until now history has been lateral (Orient-Occident, Africa-Occident, and that's leaving aside the indomitable Occident-Occident), now the earth is undertaking the cycle of multi-relation (where, beyond the cataclysms of confrontation, each singular relation will be fertilized) to its real and dense totality. It will be catastrophic for all if the distance between privileged nations and exploited peoples continues to grow. But the irreversible explodes; what Jacques Berque calls dispossession and which might better have been named the imposition of sharing. No privileged pole or rapport. Nil, depreciated. Yes: we are each in this drama the overseas of others. As is to be expected, all poetry becomes engaged, whether consciously or not. But it is true that in its calculated justness every poetics trembles because of it.

*The other of the we*

# OPEN LANDS

It was in Ibadan, in Nigeria, that I discovered and experienced what is referred to as the force of a people. That city, the most populated in Africa, extends over an infinity of little houses or cabins whose agglomeration finds its meaning in the full of the night. Then the light of street stalls, the music, the tumult and the very odors populate the night and install it in a familiar *electricity*. City of alleys and shanties, of dim lights and smoke, when, at the time, it was not unusual in that Anglophone country to glimpse (traced with charcoal on the walls or brightly painted and framed) the naive and stylized portrait of Patrice Lumumba, assassinated in the Congo. The owner of the bar that we intellectuals weren't meant to frequent at that time of night would willingly not have charged us for the local beers we consumed as long as we spoke to her of that hero already legendary in the land of Africa. She attributed to us a knowledge of the subject based on our speaking French. In the afternoon we had discoursed at the modern University of Ibadan; of European linguistic legacies; of the necessity for Africans to escape these; of ways of bringing together those in Africa who used the French language with those who spoke English. The death of an orator was greater than the sum of all of that talk.

Popular energy exploded there. Its cumulative, contained power was striking. When that mass of men will express itself, its expression will be compelling. (It is true, five years after having written these lines that energy has been diverted to the Biafran upheaval.)

It was in Nigeria that I understood what it was to have a land that carries you, invades you, confuses you. There every landscape revealed the geographic infinite to me. There are places, in Greece or Italy for example where, just as when one climbs the Florentine observatory, one feels that nature has brought together the ideal conditions for a certain search for perfection, and that there, man actually has perfected himself. But today there are places where vocation, presence, the warmth of the entire world surface: Ibadan is among those. A city without monuments but where perfection crackles in the presence of the world. Florence and the high places of Greece can close over their amphitheaters: the world there is a secret and occult representation of the self. The vast land in Africa opens onto eruption: there the world is a gigantic temptation of the Other. We islanders aren't familiar with that vertigo of the earth. We bind vertigo to its greatest tension, we must contract our space in order to live there. Our field is of the sea that limits and opens. The island presumes other islands. Antilles. The giant call of the earth's horizon is unknown to us. We could not wander without end to the ever withdrawn limits. But we forage. Our role will be to convene. The island is an amphitheatre with ocean stands, where representation is temptation: of the world.

It was in Nigeria that I was physically struck by those long-familiar voices, which marked for me the Other of the We that I am as well. The world at last.

And when one discovers (among the self, far from the self) the sudden weight of œuvres that little by little become one's own, one remains amazed by the long hardening of the *faux-semblant* of the universal. One returns to one's island. And then: *in the gigantic world we dare to have a limited experience of the sea, a challenge of smallness and concentration, an enclosed perfectibility of humanity.* I believe in small countries. And what does it matter if I want only to believe in them because my land is completely eaten by the sea and finitude. I imagine Antilles: they are there, not only destitute and isolated, but already a multiple body and radiating a lived *example*.

Such a "discovery" is already carried out first in idealism (every poet of the "birth of the world" is a Platonist: – essence!) and in chaos. Before the logic of totality suddenly invests being with its rigor and its knowledge.

(Recourse to the essence of things, to a constitutive rhythm, to the fraternity in the world, is the first lever of the absolutely dispossessed.

Coarseness. Vigor of every encounter. Unconcern when imposing an appearance on things.

Neither imperatives, nor symbolism. Nor morality.

The first temptation is to rush. The being does not first focus, *he becomes animated, emotional.* Need to fulfill centuries.

A flash of chaos that is slowly illuminated, seriated, fertilized by Measure (an active liberty).

Elementary sympathy. *Tip* of land where the relationship between man and earth is not one of *patience*. Nor the peasant's muteness nor the urbanite's muttering. The cry: deployed, or caught in the throat.

Vacancy of the earth's possession out of which a powerful desire for knowledge grows.

Chaotic tension: the inclination toward a Whole of which one wishes (since one finds oneself) to be a part.

Measure is not Reason nor simply the work of reason. It is *choice,* by which the being puts an end to his liberty in the world and offers to share in it.

The being is *suddenly* modern.
He reaches for the world but with passion.
He lives Measure Immeasurably.

The being who bursts forth with Immeasure, through struggle, grabs the right to Measure. Nation is inspiration, respiration, first.
To found one's parlance.)


Logic of totality: the weight of voices that little by little become *our* voices. As for me, abandon it from the occidental earth (earth for spirit, or spirit of an earth) and gather it in the Other America. If, on the road of our immeasurable Indies, we stopped at the shaky pier of woods, or at the irreducible stone jetties where the Discoverers muzzled their packs and perhaps installed them at the best post at the beginning of the Voyage, it was to admit that we oscillated that last time before the ocean field of new knowledge. Before the thick of self to be illuminated by the world. May the frigates, which from on high will watch over the crossing, grant us this last tremor.

*Eternal sea!* So knowledge is not abstract, and must be frisked in the field of islands as it was dreamed. Here are several voices of the We, still scattered, fragile for not recognizing one another. Three obviousnesses reinforce one another: if the first is that in the chaos of the world the fighting peoples are uncommonly exemplary (and on whom, solitary in the vow of all, acclaimed by universal will but reduced to their sole power, rests the entire destiny of relation), the second is that each must earn his calm share and the implantation of his being to be an actor of totality, and the third that perhaps the mass of a new man figures in the opacities to come: but that this man should not be a *type*. Neither does the One prevail, nor even the unique, nor unity. Totality fractures and realizes them. Out of the predictable echo of his multi-relation surface some of the underground voices that spell the future labor.

The expression is striking: with reference to Matta, the turn "psychological morphology" is used, thus signifying that at the outset the painter intends to convey states of consciousness, not to be seen but to be felt; and not in their relation to writing but *morphed* into lines and forces, colors, and flashes. He doesn't use given forms or symbolic representations, he strives to create a graphic language from the chaos and the tension of the world. Without ever altering its means, painting surpasses the narrow plastic juncture, charges itself with "significance": with the very force of matter. From this attempt at a psychological "Form" (at the same period as a psychology of form was in fact being developed) to the *Natures* and the vision, for example of "Forêt" (1956), not ever was the painter distracted from his quest for a language of depths. Matta carries in him the force of an exacerbated land (a stranger to secular labor): he could but be available to such a scarcely tranquil search, to its very secrecy.

It was a matter of *recounting* being, in its motion, its intimate trepidation, its storms; to supplement the infirmities of spoken languages which cannot offer the vision of that which lives obscurely *all in one piece*. On Matta's canvas, the gaze no longer explored space, space entered into thought. No, it invaded and encircled it at the same time. Matter's exertion to signify space, which is to say thought as well.

*"Elle inonde"*, *"Initiation"*, *"Listen to living"*: language (sig-nification) is defined by contraction and motion; an attempt to contract beings of consciousness each apparently struggling in relation to the other, or of apparently contradictory thoughts: clarity or mystery of initiation, concentration or radiation of what is alive; the very motion born of those contractions, itself a prey to vertiginous immobility. By which the spaces of Matta uproot us, seize us: making us, fixed before the canvas, sensitive to our own movement. The forces of Hatred and Love swirl in *Le Vertige d'Éros*: we enter into our most secret disorientations.

At this moment the language sought and created by the painter has found its force but not yet its style. Syntax is not a series of logical articulations (Matta proposes the "Disintegration of the thus") but foremost a relation to the other, after having become aware of his presence: a communication. Such a permeability to "others" is necessary for newly exerted language to become organized into a message. Little by little does man surface in Matta's world, spectator and actor, the presence that sanctions.

Let us follow the course of this "Spectator" (as the painter would have said). Toward the left of the canvas, "La Terre est un Homme" and all the way around the central light there are already surges, like chaotic births, expressing the identity boasted by the title. The earth is a man and every man is a tormented land, whose light it would be vain to address in the manner of a luminary. Sur-ging world where rigid flourishes are inconceivable.

Here space is eruption, the human is immeasure, thought is still chaos, but the light is already that of dawn.

Very quickly this presence, a force, takes form. Because he encountered the masks of New-Ireland, or because a man who is so subjected to the throes of the *shock of intimacy* does not remain indifferent before the conflicts that inhabit men, Matta makes *characters*. Creatures with chops (ripping apart apples or monstrously crying that they are kings) confronted endlessly with the outside, and voracious to confront it; the pulsating characters of his American period, made desperate by their inability to communicate, projected nonetheless and without restraint into a common space. "Being with", "Octrui", "However", so many titles that we would be remiss in ascribing to the gratuity of word play. This fantastic, aggressive morphology exposes our appetites and excesses.

"I made characters," says Matta, "to *climb aboard* the train of other people's vision." Understand from this that he went from intimate exploration to the analysis of the most frenzied and the most unconscious visions of each man. Space is the place of projection that must be captured.

From this naturally followed what is referred to as the period of *political consciousness*. I know of nothing as significant as these three of the painter's lines, thrown, offered, consumed (from a letter to a friend):

> *The degree of solitudes.*
> *The radiance of the misfortunate.*
> *Dawns.*

From the problem of communication (attested to by *However, Being with* and the other canvases from the *Conflits* period) to problems of solidarity (*Les Rosenberg, Contre vous assassins de colombes*), the connection is continuous. The same pitfalls before opacity, the same dismemberment, the same hope. Space is the place of suffering that must be resolved.

Thus is the organic unity of being aggregated: space and thought, communion and alterity, suffering and dawn. So Matta, by means of another growth, attempts to root the human in creative *Nature* where, beyond what is given, the gaze deposits efflorescences. For it is not so much a matter of showing the trees as of making the tree into the site of a community. When it is necessary not to paint nature but, for the painter, to travel in his nature (in nature's resolve as it inhabits him) "for the extraordinary calculation of his kind", one understands that beyond the tree he goes directly to the function of the tree: beyond vegetation to its first operation which is germination.

Such is the meaning of these paintings: New Lands. Note that the colors are more gentle as if to support the certainty that Matta knows that he finally possesses the *place* of his message, the style and basis of his language. Of course he paints with greens here, that are appropriate to the tree and the leaf. But the very splendor of *L'espace de midi* and the fire of that masterpiece, *Dar la luz sin dolor*, seem distinct from the acid flamboyance of the preceding periods and catch more fundamental mysteries off guard. Germination, dew, the work of pollen, what is birth, dawn, what carries hope and what is space before space, foundation and root, this now is deployed and *becomes visible*. *La Guêpe*, whose sting we will momentarily fear, now appears in its beneficial function as costume and mystery, flower and origin, created as much as it is creator. "Nature likes to hide" says Heraclitus. Let's leave nature when she charms us with appearances, secretly seek the vow of her service, by which she reunites us. Space is the site of serene correlations that must be sung.

Matta's roads, roads leading to the other; roads of deep language. The painter is able to tame the inconsequences he first suffered. Thus is land a force that doesn't stop projecting itself but soon finds its own meaning. It seems to me that as a painter Matta lived, and it seems to me, dominated modernity's contradictions. What he proposes in the end is a dialectics of forms and beings, and this dialectics becomes the *very subject* of art. It is not formal (mechanically posed) but lived. To the attempts at "psychological morphology" were added the temptations of the other. Always dramatic temptations. When one has experienced them, what was a search becomes an affirmation: vow and passion. Here a pictorial language is then developed, away from being without form, uniformly "formed" representations, and far from unsignified beings.

Newness of the man who made possible this work. This newness is suitably that of a continent destined more than any other to synthesis. Of everything that assails us in the world, here is a world ready to undertake unitary accomplishment. There the universal *is a given*. This New World, even though it is sometimes murky and stagnant, is like a confluent, disengaged from the constriction that can paralyze a spring. With Matta, it proposes and demonstrates this contradiction of the other and the same, those renascent forms, those realized unions, that invasion of space at last, whose forces, multiplied daily, use and transport us.

(Calculate the "impact" as well: the measure by which such a pictorial effort found, accomplished, its fundamental subject.)

One of Matta's most frequent themes is the incarnation, much more than the representation, of motions more often considered to be contracted, brazen, aggressive, tortured, "constitutive" of the psychology of modern man.

The word "incarnation" is in fact as inappropriate as the term "psychology". It is a matter of following, or of preceding, this upheaval which enables the consideration today of the man himself, the place and factor of all values, as a *composite*, much more open, struck, contaminated, than one might have thought. Vertiginous projection of the forces that fashion him, deport him beyond all "psychology".

To strip man of his coverings and throw him, flesh against flesh, into his renewal.

Matta trusts *profusion*. Profusion is the unconfused sign of what is born, surges forth. Maturity, in the restricted sense that introduces old age, protects itself from profusion. This maturity is stingy, governs and chooses, orders and fixes. Matta, who intends to surprise man in a new *birth* (at a time when he is invaded by tidal forces at last *projected* by the open world), thus mobilizes the unadorned richness of profusion. Mobility is indispensable to the conduct of the œuvre: one can only impede its energy, still its simmer by abdicating the ambition of daring what will be. It was impossible for the sacred, that inspiration of repose, that transcendence of what is, to intervene here.

Flashes, piles, material, prodigious matter, profusion prohibiting the system, the pause, meditation or explication. But one must take stock and estimate its depth. The painter did not choose his discourse, he did not accompany his œuvres with a series of "explanatory" paintings. Sculpture is the sign that enables him to mark his position on the road.

Fixity suddenly intervenes in profusion, its evidence formulated in gestating language, and the "basic drawing", which is almost always present in Matta's work as the elementary sign of confrontation, fixes itself for us in space. Yes, for acting thus as the coverings of the primordial drawing, the sculptures do constitute a miniature lexicon that one can refer to in order to better penetrate the vertigo of the painted œuvre. But here again, Matta encircles the successive approaches of confrontation which, according to him, govern art and command the relationship between others and the world. One follows in detail the forms (the compact screen for example, strained to its limit, and which, from one sculpture to another, becomes torn, holed, is transformed into an aggressive lasso of an irremediable necklace to finally become the *open bind* from the same to the other) a dialectics of surge and retreat, the modes of projection and contraction, the symbolism of the couple, unity in action.

That the artist loses us in the deliberate web of his "disordered words". That he invokes, as motors of his œuvre, the struggle against injustice, violence as wealth, hatred as ferment, History as nutrition, Revolution as Poetics: these are "moments". Their gestation must be followed from a greater (at a closer) distance. What will come must be apprehended: the man, the new man, now equivalent to the new world. Let us not catch in the trap of disparateness laid for us by the creator of forms. He plays in depth, he depopulates artistic prudence, he compromises us with him in the apparent disorder. But his intention is there.

If the painter is lucid enough never to lose sight of it, we spectators, who should also be actors, let us sometimes refer to the lexicon, the fold, the evidence – but fluid, operative, *moved* – that are his sculptures: we will learn that with Matta the governed disorder of forms opens onto dramatic alterity, not insouciant deregulation).

The sun that animates living and inanimate masses, the sun that will one day extinguish itself, creates fugitive beings: these are shadows. Through the shadow, man and beast, tree and mountain attach themselves to the vibration of an elsewhere. There is no opposition, as it is claimed, of the collapse of a fractureless light and the nuance of mottled light beneath foliage. In the most torrid desert, where no surge of life solicits the sky, one feels, in the very shimmer of the air, that inside light its opposite principle awaits: inside blinding clarity the temptation of the shadow.

Cárdenas's sculpture is *solar*. Each of its high black steles, which he elevates toward an imperious source of heat, names its shadow, that extension by which it roots itself in space. Maybe even more than a black plinth, each of these white marbles solicits a carpet of dusk in which to sink. It is not, inasmuch as alabaster, here truly whittled *in* its transparency, which carries in itself the shiver of its obscurity.

Here a sculpture not only fulfills space, it trembles there. I don't see an emptiness that the sculptured piece has come perfectly to fill; it is the piece itself, the creation that elicits around its necessary body a space no less inevitable; that extends, far from me.

Around a high totem (these steles are totems), I imagine the red, immobile bagasse of a desert; implicated in the marble I see the root of a forest that covers it over, unveils it. On this unstained marble I feel the deposit of leaves, in a distant consumed future that already protects this matter and guarantees its limpidity as early as today.

Cárdenas's universe radiates from his particular sun, evoking for us, here, already, centuries and centuries. A phenomenon in the world of invented forms, this is a universe, the immediate apprehension of which reveals the uniting of the organic, shadow and clarity, patience through matter, the inexhaustible alliance of what is torrid and what is nocturnal. A universe too that illuminates its past, exalts its eternity: these decomposed leaves that I imagined on the marble, that erosion in which the artist's polish has replaced the expectation of seasons, those vines that I glimpse growing along the totems, all of that is Cárdenas's memory, his obstinate excavation. Regardless of the material he is working (wood or marble, the creped black of surging bodies or the stubborn white of crouched bodies) Cárdenas recounts a legendary history. He is in a story.

That, after having sacrificed so much to revelation, art must now know itself with a sort of patience is a sign that, after having crudely reflected history or naively attested to history, it tends today to enter into the debate, to split off from itself; so much does the fugitive burst of inspiration lean henceforth, and lean itself, against the clear and opaque intention of a "time" and a becoming.

It seems that in such a debate sculpture would be disarmed, and radiant. Mute as to the prestige that painting or poetry can suddenly unleash; solid, total, for the patience and confrontation perceived there. In Cárdenas's œuvre, one immediately feels the dry presence of historicity.

Not that it manifested such and such event; this is best left to the exegetes of the real. Nor did he determine the dating, or chronology by which each of his œuvres would easily have followed the pretext of a pathway. The sculptor leads us to the edge of a very actual light: as though he had recuperated *some thing* from the depths of time to give it to us.

A recuperated universe, a burned memory, a future that stirs beneath our eyes: the history of men. Such is Cárdenas's justice: propriety of the motif, legitimacy of the search, "open" actuality of the œuvre, wise and confident tenacity of he who perhaps glimpses other spaces, other suns. "Significant" sculpture, which makes explicit its morality and its becoming. Fluidity of this very concrete art for animating without hesitation what could be called a "spirituality".

It is not enough to say that Cárdenas is Cuban, of African heritage. There is indeed the indication of this memory which I have mentioned. One sees the passionate connection, the tide of time, that sun and that shadow in the clay, and the will to *continue*, from the first blackened wood.

But what surprises: the sculptor's decision to assail these originary details, to rotate his material, by alternation or diversity. In this again, he keeps time. When he says: "I want to attempt horizontal totems", I can sense that for him it is not an artist's capriciousness but a necessary exploration at the edge of his forest. Maybe, beyond the periphery, a new field presents itself, trimmed for clearing. Perhaps the damned blacksmith of old tales is already joining tomorrow's available worker. Cárdenas is at a crossroads: he harmonizes a fabled heritage and a modern tension.

None could determine the nature of that *something*. Since the sculptor is not content to offer it to us, but transmutes it, works it, and orients it into our perspectives. He does not enclose himself in the absolute of closed conquests. Let us not enclose him in categories. Let us see him instead in the cited antiquity of red mud, of plains where peoples are suffering, in the future metropolis. What he procures, beyond perfections and beauties, is the consent of the other. Open worlds, concerted work, shared knowledge.

The surge on the one hand (totems), retreat and concentration on another (marbles), are inseparable from a *ventilation* of matter: because there are, of course, breaches in the sculpted volumes; but also that spiralling abandon, of the self, of circling motion, uniting totems and marbles, resurfaced busts and great burned trees, butterflies so light in their mass and their heads caught in the stone cloak. This world participates in the *stretch* which, in sculpture, is perhaps the art of conjecture. And develops at the same time in the *curvature*, the marking of which, set off with bones, thorns, hard or elegant festoons, attests here to growth and fertility. One might thus say that, always, Cárdenas's sculptures *continue*.

This silent art speaks for me, for you. If I say that it is legendary, it is because of its African breath, yes; but even more for the quiet defiance to pressing time, for the unfailing presence and the shadow beneath the foliage. Consider its slow advance from the first night, watch how it denies disintegration and achievement. Watch how it assembles *the memory of the future*. All legend is calm. And the sun one day will be extinguished. – But the shadow of man, thus bequeathed to us by Cárdenas, will have touched more secret planets.

# On opacity

The fascination imposed by Faulkner certainly doesn't come from a "density of characters": the literary (critical) dynamic has long since ceased to be satisfied by such rudimentary reasons; and the average reader is wily enough to know that character ruses aren't impressive anymore. It is in their round (in the consensual necessity of their mortal relations), not in their distinct acts, that the characters of *Absalom! Absalom!* turn (fashion) their weighty and indistinct presence. Moreover, what Faulkner is able to describe for us, by means of *human beings intricated* in a mutual problematic, is a *landscape*. It seems to me that the forest of *The Bear* is the most dense I have ever encountered in literature, and I am not sure that its description (real: "vegetal") carries over more than a dozen pages in the text. The inextricable and chaotic logic of the characters *describes* the forest. In other words, Faulkner's characters are not dense with psychology, but by their attachment to their glebe: to their fatality, their injustice, their tragic silt, their barbarism. The violence of the Western, puritan hypocrisy, imperialist mechanics aren't enough to convey the incalculable pressure for which the United States make themselves responsible with regard to the world, without the addition of the near metaphysical vertigo out of which bandits, errants, unnaturals, outlaws, parvenus, slave-owners, Indian killers and Negro lynchers began to grow. And because the Faulknerian character is the only one in all of North American literature to be *in no way* separate from his vertiginous destiny, he is the only one to totally signify the United States in their fundamental drama and in which the United States refuse to recognize themselves. Bayous, marshes, wheat plains, contraband counties, small-towns with sheriffs, country-clubs, and even the imposing metropolises never exposed in the œuvre but profiled on the horizon (for example during the chase carried out by Jason in *The Sound and the Fury*): yes, the landscape here is father and son to the character, who *exposes it*.

And since the beings in the Faulknerian universe are indissociable from their surroundings, Faulkner, behind the veil of irony or cold-blood, is indissociable from the drama he exposes also. I mean that none can ever be certain that this writer wasn't a racist, and there is still some fascination in presuming this forceful intelligence to be antiracist and struggling with the repressed obscurities of that nature marked by racism. In other words, one way or another, every American experiences vertigo, one of whose components is racism: by killing Blacks, by exterminating in the name of a "free world" or, like Faulkner, by taking charge dramatically of the *opacity* of the Other for the self. The opacity of the Negro is of course for Faulkner, his impenetrability: as black as the skin is the soul obscure. It is thus true that he was only ever able to evaluate the black man from outside, even in *Intruder in the Dust*, and even more with regard to the mulatto of *Light in August* (Faulkner succumbs to the unconscious prejudicial movement against mulattoes or mixed-blood people: the "pure" Negro is always more noble for him, and at any rate more "sound" than the mulatto). The internal monologue will never be appropriate for the black character, and what we will find there most often will be a grumble, and not conducts but series of attitudes. There is more "truth" on this point in the detective novels of Chester Himes than in Faulkner's black characters. Why then these characters, given the irritation provoked for example by the "attachment" of the old black servant to the "Family" by which she is exploited (we are all too familiar with that odious usage of the *da*), do they hold our attention? Precisely because they reveal negativity: because of the impossibility, in which the author who created them finds himself, to go into the depths of their motivations. They thus oppose to Faulkner himself a *not-beyond* into which he will never cross. In other words: Faulkner's inability to apprehend this character is *positive*. It signals that the author's enterprise is integral and absolute at all stages; and also that the American Black opposes a real density (that which was yet in America to be affirmed). But this *opacity* is terrible, and America cannot want to recognize itself there: it would be to admit a fundamental barrier: to touch with one's finger one of the gates of barbarism. And the only possible remaining operation (converting brute opacity into consensual, mutually exercised opacity) really no longer is, in which the White refuses to *conceive* of the Black, if it means killing him, and where the Black found himself reduced thus far to the ambition of becoming *mixed with* the White. Yet such is the force of Faulkner's opacity, invading the whole system of enunciation, all of which hinges imminently on this opacity, offered to a tragic enterprise of unveiling.

It is thus far from Faulkner's text, having overlooked almost everything of the articulations and incidents through which this text sinews that I want in turn (in my usage) to undertake the unveiling of this unveiling: to seriate the mechanism by which this collective American vertigo is translated at the level of literary creation, into the vertigo of the veiled struggle with its unveiling. That is all there is: the veiled, the unveiling. The affirmation first of a secret, something hidden, a *fundamental trace*, the operation then by which one attempts to reveal them (to oneself), less in their clear truth than up against the vertigo of this operation. In other words:

here there is no unveiled. No certain "reason". The unveiled would have introduced a solution of vertigo, which Faulkner will repeat everywhere is not yet *in view*: it is too early for it to intervene. The solution, in the irreducibility of his *definitions* would have put an end to vertigo, which is one of the elements of the collective being. Accordingly, Faulkner is not far from believing (metaphysically?) that any solution (to a racial problem for example) would be a negation, a deep impoverishment of that collective being. Alas! To delay the solution is to give a chance to the being to continue to tremble. But affirming at the same time the original secret and exploding a mechanism of its unveiling is to revive the collective consciousness, to maintain it in a state of anguish and questioning. The novel unveils something veiled that never becomes *purely unveiled* but *exposes itself* in the very mechanism of unveiling. It assails, fills the consciousness which reveals itself to be anxious and sanctions while rejecting it. There is no lack even of this supreme dialectics, which is that for Faulkner, and almost without fail, the victim of the occult, of the first sin (the expropriated Indian, for example) will be intermixed with the expiatory that will take on the sin. The Indian and the Negro, relegated victims of crime will also be the elected victims of expiation. The White man traverses this history as a sort of trembling *agent*. But if he is not ever a victim (for he can give back what he gets, and in the thick of his decline, precipitate an arrogant Stutpen into an apocalyptic death), he is also the *witness* (alert consciousness): contaminated by the fact of revelation more than by the revealed content; sometimes beaten down, consumed, in the fever of vertigo. To himself, he is obscure; he only understands himself through the evocation of his crimes and in the presence of his victims.

Opacity thus extends and applies not only to the enunciation (to the history of the victim and spoliator) but to the witness. Here, the witness is not the one who *tells* the story but the one who collects and recounts it. Not Miss Rosa but Shreve, in *Absalom! Absalom!* The storyteller is innocent: he only has a sort of distant astonishment and is sometimes flustered before the monstrosities he relates. In fact, the storyteller is often a woman whose energy and purity fashion innocence, and consequently *preserve* it; or else he's half-way a stranger, just insightful enough or engaged enough to understand what is going on without being contaminated by it. *Contamination* is reserved for the *recounter*: the one who disseminates the story; the latter is the true witness. Almost always a child, or an adolescent, invaded, controlled, acted upon by the mechanics of unveiling. The most complete case is that of Shreve, of whom we learn (in a dry chronology) that he died in 1910; that is, the same year when Miss Rosa recounted to him the vast history of the Stutpens. Whatever Shreve's role may be, he remains the delirious guy whose fever was set off by the fire of the old woman's revelations. Sometimes the child (a child) takes the place of the storyteller (he grows up with and in the story to be unveiled), and we must concede that in such instances the author himself takes the place of the recounter: opacity extended all the way to him. The œuvre trembles, in this instance, in the contradictory energy in which the author finds himself *caught*: in the vertigo of contamination and the lucidity of writing. Balzac, Proust, Faulkner know this duality, this tension, this tremor in and of the œuvre.

(Thus opacity encroaches on the mechanics, the technologies of unveiling: to *thicken* it. For unveiling has as its mission, not so much to deliver a truth, we have said as much, as to maintain an anxiety, vertigo. The only certainties are that at the beginning of this vast related story, there was an irreparable sin, symbolized by the stranglehold on the earth, and a solution will intervene in the end – but when and what form will it take? Between these two extremes, scandal and vertigo. The unveiling of these technologies serves instead to accelerate, like a whip the spinning top, the inconvenient inebriation of beings. In the exemplary mechanics of *Absalom! Absalom!* and despite the symbolism of the title, is it possible to say that the old Stutpen and his son, Henri (and consequently, Shreve, the witness), are horrified by the possible union between Judith and Bon because they come from Stutpen or because Bon is black by his mother? Opacity, vertigo of unveiling.)

Because there is neither a solution to put into practice nor a resolution by which to be fortified, all that is left to operate is the metaphysics of expiation. The community in its vertigo, the landscape in its excess, time in its uncertainty, Faulkner vows them all to this irrefutability. Schema: witness, unveiling, contamination. Actors: agent (spoliator), victim (original or expiatory), conciliant (distant and problematic). Significations: obscurity of sin, opacity of the heroes, fluidity of the future. Modalities: mortal vertigo of the witness, technical vertigo of unveiling, metaphysical vertigo of the contaminated surroundings. The expiatory (the Black or the Indian) is in turn opaque because there is no end to having to understand why he doesn't stop putting up so. Indeed, if we understood right away, expiation would stop there, the Negro would replace the muteness or the mutterings of nobility with language and the act of revolt (the Intruder would become Malcolm X), and the metaphysical solidarity between himself and the spoliator would collapse. It thus seems that for Faulkner there may be a "North-Americanity" more precious than justice, and gradually perfectible without the intervention of "strangers": just as the Yankees have no vocation to intervene in

Southern relations. Malcolm X could not have agreed. But if Malcolm X *chooses* his name, where the Intruder is subjected to his own, the opacity of Malcolm X is very much that of the Intruder, internalized, taken into account, *opposed*. One and other throw the average American back into the essential solitude that is his own, each time that at home or in the world (in Viet-Nam, Columbia or Brazil) he forces the recovery of his irreversible genesis: the obscure and puritanical shame of deracination, the throbbing need to affirm oneself to be "civilized"—that is, ancient, patent, stable—and the concern for legitimizing not only the right to one's land (a re-rooting) but also the privilege of *leading the world*, a privilege reserved for adventurers *who have succeeded* and who consequently hold *virtue* and *receipts*. Degenerate form of universal will. Beyond its political and economic elements, there is a fascination with oppression; and despite so many scholarly, austere, sensitive individuals, this naive, ignorant, implacable vertigo continues unendingly to expand to the dimensions of the world.

Faulkner was unable to grasp that expansion. It does not tremble in his œuvre. It even seems as though he strove to deny it, and that the minute county of Yoknapatawpha only contends to be a micro-universe in order to better refute the universe. Thus, Faulkner, who shares an obsession with the past characteristic of the nationals of the New World, is absolutely ignorant of the rest of the American continent. (One would need to determine whether it is by puritanical prudence or to muddy the tracks that Bon's mulatta mother is declared to be Haitian in *Absalom!*). No such solidarity outlined here, as weapon nor as wealth: South America is decidedly a "reservation". There lies the weakness. Installed in his solitude, the Faulknerian hero (witness and victim) is cut off from the world. It is true, moreover, that North America has more and more difficulty conceiving of the world other than "as a domain to scour, with Indians at the gates of the forts." Had it opened onto an American continent of solidarity (and no longer exploited), Faulkner's work might have enriched the future relation with irreplaceable scope.

He proves: that opacity is fundamental to unveiling; that opacity, the other's resistance is fundamental to his knowledge; that only in opacity (the particular) does the other find himself to be knowable. Lastly, that unveiling is the very principle of the Tragic; and that opacity, submitted to unveiling, presumes slowness, accumulation, duration.

# THE VOICE OF EARTH

The inability to write does not arise from a drought, from one part of the trajectory of a being having exhausted in himself all marvels and phantasms, – no more than it stems from anguish (the impossibility to order or disorder forms) – but, in our case, from a hesitation before the decisive act, which, in the literary order, consists also of building a nation.

Here we are confronted with the necessity, not, whether genuinely or not, to sing the popular wisdom that grants us authority, but to assemble a common will, by which we might be forged. Here the œuvre is not limited to translating the surroundings that comprise it; it arms and deepens itself by supporting and unveiling those surroundings, authorizing itself nonetheless and feeding from it.

This is why we have no need for successive works that hail or prophesy, but, in the margins of a creative act proceeding from it, of meticulous logic, of the patience for clearing ground, of the relentless search for a root: of a literature (preceding? – the works).

At the moment at which one discovers that the œuvre is not satisfied with reflecting its surroundings (inasmuch as those surroundings are uncertain, threatened, tracked in their existence and in their savor by those who oppose them, dominate or undo them), but must compose itself bit by bit within the surroundings, that is be born with them, illuminate the progress of their growth, signal the progressive conscience of a common existence – yes, at that moment, the œuvre ceases to entertain with other works the usual relationships from which a literature is generally formed: it is no longer out of the existence of works that literature is born, it is out of the exigency and the vital necessity of a literary conduct (intention, direction) that in our view (for now) the works proceed.

We run the chance of a literature that predetermines, by its functional investigation of a common conscience, the works that will illustrate it.

It accounts for the situation of the being, who emerged from a nation whose existence is not yet *recognized* by the nationals themselves nor, all the more so, by those who contest them.


That a literature may pose itself, before the works that will "compose" it are made – is that not a challenge? Is that proposition not governed by the most summary idealism?

In order for a literature to be "willful", that is, for it to fix for itself a subject, none can deny that a number of inconveniences will result therefrom.


The *parti pris*, which reduces and scleroses, which will obliterate savors, denature the fruits of the earth, drown the flourish beneath the tyrannical rush of too general an intention, one which may prove to be erroneous.

Error, precisely. For it is quite rash to claim to force the truth, or, further, the savor of a country, toward the totalization of expression, even if that expression (that is, self-knowledge and recognition by the other) is vital hereafter.

The sterility, finally, that sometimes comes from too mechanical a series of projects, from too monotonous a theory of realizations, a deficiency of spontaneity, or an agony of the "heart".

But sterility is pushed back by the flood of a once little known history, which, as it is unveiled, fertilizes being with a rush of unsuspected possibles, of new hopes. Inasmuch as one hesitates before the field of a history yet to be conquered, inasmuch as one resists the right to shared expression, powerlessness obliges us to quibble over trifles, when we should have been deracinating mornes.

*Collective memory* is our urgency: lack, need. Not the "historical" detail of our lost past (not that alone), but the resurfaced *depths*: removal from the matrix of Africa, bifid man, the refashioned brain, the hand, violent, useless. An absurd obviousness – where misery and exploitation are married to some derisory thing – and where, perceptible only to us, the apparently stakeless drama is played out, for which we are incumbent, presently, to make it into a fecund Tragedy.

(But what is all of this in the drama of the world?)

The meticulous reporting of dates and facts masks the continuous motion (arduous signification, which we often refuse for ourselves) of our past. To forget everything of one's history: such grace is denied us, for we have not learned a thing.

The incense of earth is in the earth
The rut of humus of rock the false summer
in their labor have gathered
roots, your haloes

we have left our heroes

they neglected our seaboard work
suave their blood rose
all night in the guano.


(All night: the first. But how many times recommenced? How many times the discovery of the new land, the sunset over the land, and the same rise in absence and oblivion?)


Wrenched from the matrix, that is where oblivion begins to suppurate, no, deracinated memory, the being uprooted from its lives, the white sea day after day impossible but still there. Sea to traverse, between the real and memory. A people preyed upon by vertiginous oblivion. The more resistant, indeed, the more capable (*the higher priced*), an elite, a selection, the depository of that human agitation where Trade did its work. Here, *the elite was always what was most profitable to the transporters.* May we hate that elite. But a people also of the vanquished, which cannot regain the surge of being other than on the mornes where several were huddled: the maroons.

Yet the real is not *beyond*: it watches from inside the threatened imminence of being. The sea is in you. It's up to you to *rejoin*, over oblivion. We have no consensus. Not broken, worn. The more authentic become mad with powerlessness and solitude. Seriate that madness.

Unveiling. Durable, patient, heavy weight, when the being projects beyond himself, in the crossed-out past that is but the paralyzing whiteness of the present.

Vain weight, and solitary: not armed with everyone's vow. Necessary, even if you paddle alone on the sea to cross. Illusory, but unfailing. We all crossed the sea, all must remember.

Unveiling. Tragedy: extracting from oneself to find strength in the self. The unveiled that has come to consciousness or rather to the total being, introduces (besides the vertigo of its operation) a solution of utter immediacy: the community of the nation. A poetics: the share in everyone of reconquered duration.

The poetics of errance is interwoven with violence without a cause. Oriented violence becomes a politics of rootedness. The poetics of rootedness is an arduous reflection on absence of cause.

Drama of the intellectual: the complete range of illusions (of the self) will never be worth the assent of a single cane cutter. Intellectuals *believe themselves*. That is why, sold or pusillanimous, ostensibly free or false criers, they always serve those who exploit cane. (Their class of literacy was created with this aim).

The usury of the collective soul is such that one can but unsettle the soul, profoundly. By whom was such usury exerted? By intellectuals, created.

The obscure desire for identification with a false father (who took the place of the fallen mother) finds in each elect his equivalent: with the clear desire to be the immemorial father. Cesarism is the temptation of the deracinated.

The community, the memory in all, the œuvre of unveiling, the hastening of the Nation first presumes aggression (which is the real signification of a no) against the false father, false Cesars.

The poetics of duration opens also onto every fortune of the expanse: I can see Saint Lucia to the south, Dominica to the north: I imagine what will follow. Every island contributes to the unity of this sea.

Our obsession with the past wants only to be illuminating. Our weakness in the present sometimes appears to us as a fragile preservation of communities to come.

All willful literature anticipates, and defends itself against prophetism. Stands firm in being, and can want but the All.

To the trauma of removal corresponded the trauma of "liberation". Procured (or consented to) civil rights never replace *the Name one has chosen for oneself*. The deracinated slave is succeeded by the depersonalized citizen. Finding one's person again is a dramatic act, which is not without difficulty.

What is referred to here as order (preserved at *any* price) is the terrifying nothingness in which a stained illiterate society attempts to maintain a people without reference.

Every poetics is a search for reference. Reference *only occurs* when those it concerns are imprinted by it without exception.

(Reference is total).

A voluntary literature postulates reference, obliges itself not to delineate it.

Reference is of totality.

Thus does collective exigency mature.

To encircle a common project, driven into the most secret and sometimes most reticent part of each individual.

This drama plays itself in and around us: of a being (the Antillean) who is not yet recognized as such and who tries, in each of us, to cry out. Drama of that existence, certain, imperative, nonetheless fragile, ceaselessly threatened. Drama of the imminence of a people. This people *is*, it does not speak. (We who speak are not its voice). It does not live. (And we are not its breath).

Cries we have uttered for more than three centuries, from that cartage of living matter that seems endlessly to be engulfed by a mouth of the void, making a systematic selection, in order perhaps to draw out what was missing from the cry in order to become parlance. From the passional or diffuse impulse that batters our lives, disengage the one and operative consciousness of our being.

At the highest pitch of our real, to know, not only the cry, its beauty, its truth, but even the zones of impenetrable silence into which the cry has dissolved. To attempt, beyond our weaknesses, to reestablish that *continuity* that betrayed us so, and whose absence is the means by which a cry eternally initiated ultimately becomes fixed in the complacency of its echo. To know what, in us and around us, imposed such paralyzing discontinuity.

Regarding discontinuity, elect the composite. The composite is one of those ideal givens of modernity, each time it is organic and just, in other words when it doesn't require of man that he amputate himself of even one of his values in despicable favor of another.

That a consciousness precedes the state (the body, collective, in its manifestations and its patents) that will assume it, such is one of the characteristics of our situation, which is rendered possible as much by the lacks and vicissitudes of our history (this unwitnessed struggle) as by the progress of knowledge. More belated (more "constructed" and more constrained) than the other peoples, we are not born of a slow work of aggregation but literally into the consciousness of our necessity. Consciousness seems to precede the total body, but it is from being, each time imminent, in the gehenna of history, that consciousness dawned. A composite, scattered, but inevitable people, a culture, innervated, diffuse, but particular and avowable, slowly explode in the unavowed consciousness of their being.

Literature: experienced through that anticipated consciousness, while still stammering, if one only considers the formal reality of what will comprise it. Not codified, since it will result from the effort of the collective body that we aren't yet. And systematic, since it requires the work of consciousness which, in us, is not (there) explicit, but urges on.

For those who haven't any of the means by which continuity exerts itself (nor language nor art nor community), folklore constitutes the only field in which the common goal is inscribed. Fecund and rich when it is assumed in immediacy, folklore otherwise becomes a purring alibi. It only grants joy, open to all without mediation, when evident and signified collective consciousness allows it to continue at the level of culture, in other words of the acceptance and enrichment by all of a heritage recognized as indelible.

Literature: impulse of that common work, systematic and perchance gripping expression, by which this work is announced. Both the cry, transported by so much attentiveness, and parlance, which, according to its logic determines itself in a new world. The impact of the cry, the daily call, the burgeoning, and (at the same time), the continuity of conquered (not given) clarity, the critical œuvre, ripening.

The flash of the cry, the arduous opacity of parlance.

# In memory of the Niger river

When the literary project is uncertain – the literary act does not come naturally to the collective being, which is not manifest to being – the painful effort of consciousness throws into question both being and literature. The latter becomes impossible: foreign. For us, sons of storytellers – of *parleurs* – literature is a temptation: blossoming for the satisfied, worried and imperfect for the acute. The latter deny it, and make it for real: the effort of Kateb Yacine. The willful grunt tightens and grips. It happens that, in the difficult relations between the religious and the literary, we prefer, for example, rigid intrication to sumptuous display: Hopkins over T.S. Eliot. Sometimes, against the difficult passage from parlance to script, literature can seem too obvious to us in Césaire, more humble, more ingrate, less natural, and consequently (as for us, and at a certain time) more appropriate in Paul Niger. The difficulty in conceiving the literary may have played a role in our budding "literature".

I am endlessly constituting the Niger river: one, essential, damming the immense page with its fire. It must be so still, so vast, so full of worlds, of mud, and beings, I see it as the stinging and restive attribute, the major mark on an unappreciable expanse. I take what, of it, is turbid, feverish, unapproachable and sunken, and turn it back, make it irrupt. (In the word he has chosen for himself, what I first see in Paul Niger is not the symbol and the idea, but the landscape and the River).

The significance ("history") of landscape or of Nature is the revealed clarity of the process by which a community cut from its ties or its roots (and perhaps even, to begin with, from all possibility of rootedness), comes gradually *to suffer* the landscape, earn its Nature, know its country. To deepen significance is to carry that clarity into consciousness. The ardent effort toward the land is an effort in history. Here there is no given matter that is safe from the passion of time. You deport me to a new land (it is an island), you abduct from my mind and the deepest parts of myself the science of the old land, you object that the new land is yours alone, and thus must I move back through the ages, far from earth. Here then (by force of foothold) I feel the earth under my feet: I grow back immediately in yesterday, I feel around for the depths of irremediable time, I sand up oblivion and hurtle down the year, I reconquer my memory and grant value to my inspiration: such is stirring the earth and planting one's tree. (Thus begins Paul Niger: set to work and pains).

And this land: what does it signify then? Time and Space, intermixed. That its essence has died (with those last Arawaks who threw themselves, the whole tribe without exception, into that baie des Trépassés), and is reborn to a new intention: crossroads of spaces and eras. It is an island, and it is no longer one. Its sea is fordable; the horizon does not enclose. The land has ceased to be essence, it becomes relation. Essence was ravaged by the action of transporters, but relation is interred in the suffering of the transported.

Little by little the land is devolved upon those who suffered it, gave it new meaning. They know it not in its (expired) essence, but in a more capital becoming: in its vocation of receiving and going. The islands of the Antilles assume tomorrow to be divided.

Thus essence is to birth as relation is to becoming. We were not born, we were deported, from East to West. A sailor's knife cut the umbilical cord. Slave irons stopped the blood. There is no essence there, but perdition. In the relation to the new land, in the relation of that land to the sea and the environs, becoming takes stock of itself, where perdition ends.

The literary act, at that moment when Paul Niger was watching, was not to burn out far from land, but to carry those passages – of *frustrated* essence and birth in relation and *conquered* becoming – to consciousness.

Today, to carry them to the community. To those who haven't had a voice and for whom *we could not be their voice: in that we are but a part of their voices.*

# TRAGIC STRUGGLES,
# EPIC FREEDOMS

Nowhere as much as in Tragedy does the opacity of works achieve that hard radiance: each tragic cycle is a ceaselessly postponed enterprise of unveiling. The conduct of a tragedy thus ravishes the spectator from the world of the instant and installs him in duration.

"Theatre" which is not Tragedy presents itself as the expression of *a single dimension* : either of spectacle (succession of "tableaux"), or of proofs (succession of "reasons"). Tragic theatre, which falls within an art of opacity and unveiling, aims toward no effect, whether immediate or deferred. The necessity, for example, for Comedy to "signify" in the instant and to "prove" in this sequence which is but a procession of instants; the necessity, on the contrary, for Tragedy to perpetuate in duration an opaque unit of truth that it underlies.

Tragedy is opposed to Drama in that its accomplishment authorizes an even more clear situation where the original situation will have been confused and painful. If Drama is but accidental, gradually contaminating and dissolving (after which, there is nothing), Tragedy is the re-solution of dissolve. Drama plays on a situation, and worsens it. Tragedy leads to the exasperation of a tenebrous situation, whose dénouement opens onto equilibrium and clarity. Tragedy is total joy. Sequence, through the tragic, of a whole subterranean joy. A music of obscurity.

Suffering and joy, the opaque and the obvious succeed and equal one another: Tragedy is of the law, by its very nature, and besides the sacrifice of heroes, is only achieved with the advent of the Just.

The proper object of the Tragic appears to have its principle in the search and signification of a ruptured or threatened "community", which Tragedy must re-form. The great Tragic moments seem to coincide with periods, not of crisis, but of fermentation, of collective advancement. Thus of the two possible forms of Tragedy, the sacred and sacrilegious, the one that consecrates unanimity and the one that attacks convention, the first seems to be historically loftier.

Theatre is an art of unveiling, not of proposition or analysis. The Tragedian senses a consciousness in motion, which he does not anticipate; the participating public becomes the consciousness of Tragedy. Here opacity is irreducible: even when the community signified by the œuvre has long since vanished.

Comedy is "instructive", a force of attack, itself a function of a system of references. Opaque, it organizes and orders the diffuse from within, it snakes through chaos in search of equilibrium, it is embodied at every dawn of time like the flourish of becoming.

Through the tragic act, a community begins to meditate upon its own action. It is the sign of a shared possibility of action. It is consciousness beginning, received or heckled, of peoples being born to their action. It is probable that a nation will not twice nourish a great tragic cycle. A people yet incapable of its act is not familiar with tragic crystallization: a people that already *acts* no longer has need for it. There is no great tragedy without national impulse or presumption. As beautiful as tragic necessity is, its undue reverse is ridiculous.

For the Greeks, for Shakespeare, in seventeenth century France, the driving particularity of the Tragic is all-powerful Fatality. The hero shoulders the collective force, and it is out of his excavation that the final concord is born, it is out of his choice that freedom emerges. We are not willing to consent to sacrificial necessity: today man has learned not to despair of freedom (hope) to the point of sacrificing ritual heroes. The notion of fatality surrenders to that of historicity.

The Greek relation of man to his power, the Shakespearean relation of man to the world, the Racinian relation of man to himself – today, the denied people in struggle make that bind. A great tragic cycle would therefore circulate through the opacity of the relation to be perfected, of the unity to be conquered. The action of peoples newly born to the world is its first word.

Such a Tragedy would be novel: Tragedy of times of crisis, and not of slow maturation. The desirable unity would cease to be bound to national unanimity and carry opacity (the search for a common reference) to planetary dimensions.

But tragic action never takes place at the extreme of an idea – an ideology – even if it is "total" or "true". Tragic unveiling is developed from those obscure, concrete, bound forces, which tie themselves to the movements of peoples. There is indeed a necessity for Tragedy in Poetry: Poetry is the art of veiling in the immediacy of the word, of unveiling in the continuity of language. Both open to a world from prior necessity. Tragic action could however not emerge from an impossibility to act. One could not dream of a Tragedy "born of nothing". The failures attest to it: when the tragic writer does not enlarge the actions of his people (when he is alone in his drama), he carries testimony for the Whole, but not for his community in action. Today, tragic action will yet illuminate action: if opaque parlance and tragic unveiling are taken into account by each community; if the prior necessity buttresses a prior liberation.

(Meteoric revelation, the acme of the poetic instant by which the French nineteenth-century protested against classical uniformity, so dignified the act of poetry that they seemed henceforth to have combined with it. But at such a remove from a liturgy of the instant, poetry can consecrate a problematic of duration, and reinstall that knowledge at the heart of Tragedy.

Similarly, the failure of *epos* signifies nothing other than the poet's will to take history by the letter, clumsily to array the œuvre, rather than plunge into the obscure, non-unveiled sources of historical accomplishment.

Finally, if we are living in a time of crisis, where the search for a shared reference is no longer possible, a new project may nonetheless mature: it is the one that concerns relation between various references, far from an illusory and dangerous Universal.

That is a matter for another labor, perhaps a new deepening of the Tragic and the Epic, brimming over the frame of an elect civilization or culture.)

Tragedy does not affirm for the modern world the *irreducibility* of a people, but its right to share (its struggle). *Epos* will not qualify the *contrary* gesture of a people, but its relation (its true freedom).

Our necessity today: to affirm, not one community *facing another*, but *in relation to another*. In other words, the irruption of historical consciousness overturned the ancient schemæ: once, Tragedy *gathered* the epic gesture, it unveiled its consciousness to a people, which *epos* had sung raw. Tragedy-consciousness was the *represented* echo of the *epos*-gesture. Today, it is the affirmation of these peoples (the struggle to snatch the right to gesture and to parlance) that is tragic; it is freedom – the new, imposed, consensual relation – that will carry the epic. Modern Tragedy would sing the freedoms of men; modern Epos their commuted accord. Epos was once the "concrete", where Tragedy could exceed, be "abstract", "universal"; today Tragedy would be concrete, the struggle of peoples signals the obscure, bound, delivering forces, and it is Epos that, as if from the most distant of planets, will be able to circulate through the human vow to bind, to relate. Tragedy is of men and of the land; Epos will soon be of the One (again, the One, while awaiting further fracture and diversification), interplanetary.

The epic is in each of us. It is no longer an extreme moment, where the fist falls and seals a destiny. The epic wells out of us, for this that we are, each a part, this threatened whole. The world binds its parities. The sea and the land pull themselves away, toward other stars. The melee of peoples, already sporting on each head the new star that is yet to be discovered. The epic is born of us, because it will be up to us to exceed from all parts. The epic is today neither scramble nor swarm of consciousness in a people, but a perspective tendered to communal and tragic divinations. The epic, once aggregate, once solitude, today is open league, and frank and foolish prognostication.

The epic will not summarize: from the melee it *predicts* (this is prognostication: a "shared" becoming). And if the participating community is not yet consciousness (power), if its becoming is fragile, imperative but threatened – beyond the poem, the complex *epos*, and if today it is *subjective*, it will comprise the being of the community against the excedent, where this becoming is emergent.

The consciousness of the nation is thus consciousness of relation.

The expression of relation is the calculation of its negative plenitude: its prevarications, errors, denials. Objectivity cannot include these retreats: once, it was the sign of an organic and hidden push. The modern epic does not separate from the lyric: it binds and unbinds the chances of each to the field of diversity.

The brutality of surfacing, the necessity of irruption onto the stage of the world, deny dead time, beautiful meditation, the slow rise of common consent. The peoples rush down, to share in the worlds (consensual opacities).

The reconsidered self of the community is thus played out for the threatened whole of humanity.

In epic accumulation, a "naïve" period is no longer possible. Literature doubles itself: the call of concrete riches (of the vow of plenitude and knowledge) is altogether contemporaneous with the consciousness that considers and reflects the vow. The action of peoples is an unannounced source of expression.

Thus the exceeded poem is no longer a patient and sufficient catharsis. Beyond the poem lurks a *complete* expression. It forges itself everywhere: it is difficult for each to catch its echo off guard, also to weave a part of the network, *in its very language*.

Moreover two choices are sterile – ignore the total voice and its necessary internalization: of the universal vow as a schema and abstract impulse, of the imposition of the other as a fallacious mirage of the Same.

The epic is Problematic: its theme is of the future, its advent (its realized truth) can only open onto an unsuspected diffraction.

To live the relation is thus for each to wail the song of his land, and exhaustively to sing the dawn in which it *appears to itself*, and is already dissolving.

They called me to the high times
From the deep wiry throes
I forgot the form of my face.

The face of my cry is interred in the hardness of Courbaril,
Where the sea keeps watch, capsizes.

Who, which host, which master in my body granted you this power
    To cry
You cry in my body, and I have forgotten you
Are you the moon of my heart come down at midnight
Between three candles, and two are lit?

You call me your land is it your land
They have hailed me
I lived in a country arid and red

The one who has lost the Trace, he cannot undarken my face
Nor recognize it in the hollow of his hands.

*Intention and relation*

# EXCEEDING INTENTION

Where histories meet, History comes to an end. (The pathetic effort of occidental nations to remain masters of the destiny of the world, and which is vain enough for the Occident itself to split into contrary intentions, suggests to us that the intrusion of (relativizing) relation into the heretofore absolute field of History – has killed History. Thus the first man of the Occident who dreamed of another land (adventurer, merchant, priest, roughneck soldier, or poet of elsewhere) began really to assume and actually to exhaust the Occident. This acting race accomplished the field of the One and opened the world to the Relational, which it does not want to experience). We are not able, in what is each time called History, to delineate the *taste* in us, without falling back into injustice, for *one* history. I can deny History: if I am free to do so (if I am free to make it), or if, my history bricked together in the time of the One, I do not make it with the design of denying the Other.

And when Nation renders itself possible, it denies itself also: at least in that lurch of consciousness out of which we are born today. But to require of those very people who have not accomplished the One, who grew up in, with, and by relation, to require of them that they renounce the Poetics of the nation, is to ask them to amputate themselves from a past (lived through others), which must comprise a part of the fire of their present. The nation of those who had no nation in the field of the One (of those who did not make nor impose a monolithic History) must be tied to the excess of the Other. It is up to me to renounce a certain *color* of the nation, not for you to advise me of it. I am no heir to your sectarianisms, I have no fear of succumbing to them. I can go beyond the nation: if it has already been achieved in the field of the One, or whether, new or future (projectable), I conceive it as whole and carry it to the excess where relation lives. (In other words: if the men who live in and suffer the country carry the excess to the heart of the nation).

The Poem. Risen out of what depths? If it does indeed sanction and embody a poetic thought, is not every poetics today just and heavy with the conception and total activation of the diverse poetics of the world? There is no *one poem* that grants, there is no *poem* that summarizes. Poetics bore into the great auction in which the world at last reunited and diverse, is sold, tendered, reassembled. The poetics pierces the depths (does not rise out of there indistinct), demands denial where it affirms itself; from a poetics of the poetics of the world emerges an anti-poetics (a negation of the One in the field of the Diverse). The poem is the poetic tool of the One. The *noise* of the poem today is given in another noise: that total, armored, denying, binding voice. The poem is a moment of voice, it does not come to rest. It is a swath of the whole, which does not rush out of itself alone. I can surpass the poem if my voice is supported by the enormity of uncertainty, if I consent to the densities of perfection imposed by the poem; if, when leaving it, I tend to arrive at it.

What is fecund duration, when the past collides with the black pier, goes astray? Still what is duration, when, isolated, we surface from the past, drunken with the poetic weight of its structures? What good does it do you to know, if you are not flush with your surroundings, *exceeded*? Duration is worth only as much as it is accentuated in all, as We live it. The voice only rises to the circle of the possessed (of the assembled), beneath the surge of a drum and the crackling of *woods*. There is a story for you, a dying love, and a story for us, a love in death, which accepts and curbs it. The We? But it corrupts, disturbs, if, you comprehend intellect as asceticism of your knowledge. It is duration for those who hold the past, suffering, knowledge of the hide-out on the morne. Duration is share. It is the house of the We. If we deny duration: then at last we will have conquered, full and durable, the fantastic burgeoning of the instant, for all, in the joyful concern for all. Yes, what duration carries into the instant is the sacrament (the vow) of commonality. If we deny duration: we will have left the iniquity of *one* History, in order to enter into the nation, poetics, histories – commuted, labyrinthian, vital.

Intention thus perfects itself in Relation. In the related: parlance devoted to the complex state, neither to refuse nor to mask nor to blister it. In the bind: being-oneself to be the other, forever and without hope. In the relative: the negation of a History and the open dawn of histories, what accomplishes Time and hardens it there in rock, the dew-green lichen of frail inspiration and the dark stubborn rust of willful parlance, flush with the earth.

The literature, of willful being, does not cease to remain a vow. But the vow, thus supported, denies itself at last as it is realized. Willful literature destroys itself as it is accomplished. The dense vocation grafts itself by duration *into* the country's succulence. When sap is recognized as sap, it is no longer ideational; but function. When you navigate in your land with all, you no longer cry the land: you sing it and provoke it. Literature ceases to be "willful" as soon as it is "liberated". I can see us moving forward in the land, the *inspired* that we will become.

The damnation of this word: *métissage*, let's write it out large on the page.

It is foremost the *métis*, who, by tradition (as history's avatar), considers himself to be a failure. He is always (in a certain literature) ashamed of something: his parents cannot marry, they fear for his life, or else he has been abandoned by his father. The internalization of racism (always in this kind of literature) is the fact of the *métis* himself. And, always because of history's avatars (violence and hatred between two races), he is for everyone an object of scandal.

Enlarge the pathetic, individual case to our collective reality, and see how we aim to decerebrate a community, by convincing it from inside of its dried up vocation (that its ancestors denied, that it left them, that its distant father – first putative then natural – must be prayed, that dangers from all directions threaten) in sum, a bastard, it cannot be given to itself: and this community withers with the acceptance of its shame (*métissage*), for lack of promoting the value of the composite (which is not the disparate here). Neither the word nor its signified reality are to be rejected. Relation carries the universe to fecund *métissage*. Those who live that state are no longer (in their consciousness) pathetic victims: they are heavy with exemplarity. Beyond suffering, the community that *métissage* gathers cannot deny the Other, nor history, nor the nation, nor the poetics of the One. It can but exceed them.

The river was once like a delta of infinitesimal irrigations, pulpy with leeches, where the spirals of mosquitoes took on the scope of very natural cataclysms. From it (before memory was even able to impose its idealized image) I derived the dream of childhood, the desire to be. But today it is a gutter, its delta gorged, described by choring industries. The childhood Lézarde is no more. When suddenly, in the hollow of Dominica – island of a thousand rivers – I find the departed being, the fire stones, the rolling bay of transparencies, the water's caprices, the crisp cold. The irremediable oriel of this island speaks again of mornes and backwaters. On the rolling road that opens onto Roseau, the mirage of those minuscule banana hangars costumed with dry leaves, like ghosts of clarity. The dense dominant unrest of vegetation. The narrow roads gullied by cars. I find myself in this country caught on the same language, precisely the same Creole parlance: alloy. The English left fewer traces hereabout than did the French in Martinique, and at first glance there is less tension. But the island with a thousand rivers, as much as its waterless neighbor, will see its deltas dry up. In the face of Elsewhere, what price will the *métissage* of these shores not have to pay?

Soil. Darkened that I hail, that distances me, you undone from your dream of rains your mud your solitary navigation. You have this field for patient root, the sea enriches you. Here you are all started over, here, beyond. You are one among each – all islands single island – in your same density. I see you ignorant opening your space. And weak hardening. Knotted, to soften you. And each shadow on your future body, each forest of night, each human ferocity – little by little are illuminated, to open to our voices the hard delight of your spaces.

Trinidad, by which the arc seems to anchor to the continent: we dreamed there of the South that is in us. A Sunday morning in the streets of San Juan: the considerable peaceful vacuity which is neither of Providence nor of Ennui, and which we only glimpse hereabout. My house of several days, buried in the heights of Guadeloupe, where it was so adventurous to enter at night. The Cuban peasant of Haitian stock with whom I spoke in Creole (oh emotion) in the Sierra. The agricultural workers of Saint-Lucia, parked in a Martiniquan plantation. Hope is ignoble. It is language organizing itself. My land infinitely: in this field of uninvented islands.

Yet we renounce poetry when the question grips you, when on the expanse of sea you cannot discern a wave, not a single shimmer that holds you to answering. And this unformulated question – where the poem suddenly becomes silence, throbbing – is that of a being reconciled with himself at last but uncertain of his being: what is he to the other who is in him, and for the other who opposes him?

(And what is all of this in the drama of the world?)

The poet's vow is not now to abstract himself from his being, to entrust his song to strange forces that will soon smother him, nor by a contrary exercise, to withdraw into his gravity and rage lyrically at what is most desolate in himself. There is that movement by which the spectacle of surroundings illuminates (disorders), while the imposition of each parlance tends to order in the world. This double necessity, which has been the secret seed of poetry, is today articulated like a solemn law, without detour. The poet doesn't cease to obey this commandment, twice denied, twice consented to. He leaves the spark, the "revealed", that punctuation of nothings, that lure of illuminations which evaporates in the fugitive actuality of the image, to give itself to a duration in which rhythm multiplies. The poet chooses, elects in the mass of the world what he must preserve, what his song is attuned to. And rhythm is ritual force, lever of consciousness. It makes its way toward those forces: prosodic richness (rigor), guarantor of choice, guardian of conquests: the knowledge of the world in its density and its drift, the illuminating underside of History. Which is to say that poetry starts over in the epic domain. In our anarchic universe, such a manner of poetry ceases to be accidental, imposes itself as an imperious Harvest. It names the Drama that is ours: fire of the Diverse, struggle of the Disparate, vow of the

Other. In chaos, it perpetuates this work, which is that of poetry alone: to fell walls, bark; to unify without denaturing, order without taxidermizing, unveil without destroying; to know at last each thing, and this space between one thing and another, these saps, these countries – at the sharpest of the spirit and the magnanimity of the heart.

The inextricable nonetheless envelops us, inasmuch as the Old World carried its shadow over us. By reflecting our immense *range*, our self-evidences become muddied. Our clarities are offended. Our knowledges, effortless not so long ago, yield in complexity, arduousness. It seems that what grants force to the vow of poetry is that it will have to *conquer* its simplicity right up against the split injunction where knowledge has led man: to be consciousness and denied science of consciousness, language and the tongue that contests language, sign and signifier falling from the signified.

But we, drawn through this history (I see the trace left by our feet), will we inherit this injunction? Will we profit from it, without its gravity demanding it of us? In truth, no "construction" *forces* us. No cathedral. Not a single great book in common. Our history is to come. (Our poem is enmeshed with your reluctances, complicated by your conquests; but our cry is clear beneath the latticework). In what you call History, between the ditches in which our nameless heroes were interred, I see nothing but the trace of our feet.

# On a deficiency of monuments

So don't come this way, you will find no monuments. (Don't sing our land, its song is enclosed in these ditches). Our theatre was internal, its stage is against the earth: we aren't acting yet, and our actions will not comprise a play. For us, night is malevolent: nocturnal life, creator of fires and intelligence, is carefully stolen from us. In my dead city, the midnight wanderer is a voiceless watchman, surprised by his presence. The lifeless streets haven't even the charm of ancient things: our past does not belong to us. On the heights of Balata a derisory reduction of the Sacré-Coeur of Paris reminds us that we are concerned with reconstituting an elsewhere. Dis-taste governs us. *So, to open to the arduous complexity of the world. Not to an other, but to the martyred vow of the other. May the earth in chaos come to us, for light.* The favor to grant you, Western mariner, is indeed to read your œuvre *diagonally*, to apply other seas to you, other shores, other darknesses.

*Thus* out of the opacity of the world, out of seasonless suffering we surface dreaming of beauty born to misfortune. Yet we make an offering: elevated is the offering which does not disorient. For three centuries I followed the way of the West, my heart riveted to a rock that my feet had never once met.

# OFFERING

By the most distant star, I commence the offering. And I remember that I wanted to associate the argument of this book to it: between the acoma tree and the star *Fomalhaut*, I saw a same river flow through the spaces.

Weingarten is a visionary. He organizes prophetic apparitions, legendary landscapes and histories, like the enthusiast in search of enchanted Isles discovers lands and mounts.

> *I see a black tear.*
> *It looks like a tear running behind a glass, on a very grey day, and all we can do is watch it run.*
> *But on the horizon, that bar? That cloud so dark, is it the sea standing up all charged with storms?*
> *Is it the sea standing up?*

and:

> *Look oh my soul at what has become of this ancient Kingdom. What is left of this ancient Kingdom?*

and:

> *I see a man walking alone along a road. Walking straight on . . .*

These are beginnings of poems in *Fomalhaut*, in which we realize that the poet first *sees*, and asks us to *look*. Whence an apparent negligence of the "ear"; yet Weingarten organizes his "visions" with certainty, a surge that results in our being here in the presence of a style (concerted writing).

Great are the dangers. Prosodic concern can lead, by way of the plainsong, to a hackneyed poem, just as the concern with nakedness, of depth by-the-letter, can dry up or invertebrate it; thus the visionary exercise can fail in the wasteland of pseudo-realist bric-à-brac, where "envisioned" objects have no definite function anymore. But from the deep ages, Weingarten frequents the rumor of truth with which each poet struggles.

> *Listen to me, my sisters, they are speaking to me of you!*
> *The wind is a sentinel in the night*
> *And my heart keeps watch alongside yours!*

Attentive to the convulsions of being, he engages poetry in *something other than itself*. This can quickly ring false, artificial, mediocre, if the poet, as is the case here, is not *subjected* to this "other thing", as deeply as possible. We feel Romain Weingarten's effort to break the envelope, to communicate his fire, to reunite and accomplish. His poetry is not a simple "communication of words", but like an imposition of flame and ardor:

> *I will take the burning fire*
> *the cattle that's led away and that's branded with irons*
> *I'll take the last of the last*
> *and carry them in my arms*
> *and I'll emerge!*
> *I'll call my true children, my sparrows,*

212

*and my children will emerge!*
*I'll raise a new harvest*
*on the earth*
*and my king will emerge!*

Far from the grace of finery, it is time for some to perform an almost arid examination of "poetry's reasons". These are poets who strive, beneath ingrate appearances and "obscurity", for a strict rigor in the conduct of themes, toward a necessity. Paul Mayer is secret. He startles with patience and simplicity. What is his project? To give (it seems to me) a form, without formulæ: a landscape, disengaged from all horizons; a poetics without theory of the true place and out of place.

*Shreds of ships*
*Shadows of faces that disappear in ash*
*So slowly that a dream wears out in a book*
*Wingless, in the hollow of the book*
*Lie naked birds and their bodies*
*bleed in the night of pages*

The sort of dispersal that opens *La Roue des Corps* (it is difficult to produce flesh in a single flash) is followed by a gathering, a collection of images, of lights and shadows.

*Useless towers, satiate vestiges of days*
*Beneath the grapes of fire our cities are captive.*
*Only the world of the dead troubles the peace of graves;*
*The echo of words quieted by their mouths*
*Still vault the sky of a destroyed empire,*
*And night like water fills them with delays.*

The central theme comes out of the devastations of war. This pretext for writing is exceeded by the lesson of writing. (Slow, obscure words, promised to the night of death that has been traversed by the poet, in search of his order. And: out of the darkness that somber shard is secreted, which is the sign of *proclaimed unity*):

> *Angels of uncertain life on the shores of destiny*
> *The salt and our thoughts gnaw at your stone cheeks:*
> *Visitors of the profound dwellings of Gomorrah,*
> *Listen at my door, it is like the sea,*
> *And whispers in the ears of those who have nothing,*
> *Who are open, like homeless windows,*
> *To the contrite harmonies of urban seasons,*
> *Like to the July sky the arms of harvesters.*

War and the "grapes of fire" have thus left a space for hope, just as scattering preceded unity. Language and intention clarify one another mutually: a world that is full, secret, tormented also, where poetry makes itself

> *Vital and hard beneath a devouring azure.*

In *Hier Régnant Désert*, which follows the book of *Douve* (following closely from it), one does not encounter these sudden notations, as if removed from the central project, in sum these "accidents of writing", by which Douve, sculpture embossed on the night found itself enveloped with a layer of *somber shards*.

When the poet writes: "Great hounds of foliage quake", I feel as though my gaze is leaving Douve the Absent, to find her again in a more essential dwelling: the quake itself. And I see Douve penetrated by the wind, weeds, submerged by "cold heads with beaks, mandibles", radiating "a strident joy of insects", finally, "ravaged, exalted . . .", "genial, inverted". In this, Douve's body, the poem concentrates the forces of a night (which is perhaps that of death), and Douve, sculptural in that night also suffers from the night, carries it in herself like "a village of cinders". This interrogation of night that was *Douve* fed, if I may say so, off its essence: the night was in Douve, who was nothing but night.

The extent (which could only be obscure, stolen) of this double possession, is perhaps signified here in this poem which concludes the series, entitled *Douve parle*:

> *Be quiet because we too are of the night*
> *Its most formless gravitating roots*
> *And the clean matter, returning to the old*
> *Reverberating ideas where the fire has dwindled,*
> *And face furrowed by a blind presence*
> *Maid banished heatedly from a dwelling,*
> *And parlance lived but infinitely dead*
> *When the light at last has made itself wind and night.*

Is this not to propose that the forces of the night cannot be approached or known other than in silence and "blind presence", by the extinguished fire becoming "wind and night"? Yves Bonnefoy thus joined those who chose not to dominate but to "keep vigil". When he writes: "I am the master of your night, I keep vigil in you like the night," understand that here the master is not a demigod but a castaway who accomplishes the wreck:

> *I will know how to live in you, I will steal*
> *In you every light,*
> *Every incarnation, every reef, every law.*

If Douve concentrates in herself the substances of the night, it is to relieve it of the abstract "laws"; and it is also why the poet gives himself over, abandons himself to those shards, to those accidents, that materiality by which writing exalts itself. Never is this imposition of materiality denied in *Douve*. When the time comes to mark "a secret rupture" in "the night of being", the poet experiences it absolutely: "A bush surrendered". By the grace of this wounded bush appears a salamander, the somewhat "dialectical" realization of the night and the fire, of silence and parlance, of life and death. For we had understood that this night (which we said was of death) is also that of truth; that truth is not only light, life. Henceforth,

> *The sun will turn, its vital agony*
> *Illuminating the place where everything was unveiled.*

The sun, its agony. The poet answers his own interrogation: not by defining an answer but by asking another question. Without leaving the place of the dead, that night on which the obscure truth stalks us (for to leave the night we risk wounding truth), can we call day, "force and glory"? Already the poem had bequeathed to us the vanity of "lamps", but we also read this:

> *If this night be other than night,*
> *Be reborn, distant beneficent voice, awaken*
> *The gravest clay where the seed has slept.*
> *Speak: I was nothing more than desiring earth,*
> *Here at last the words of dawn and rain.*
> *But speak so that I may be the favorable earth,*
> *speak if there be yet another smothered day.*

*Douve* closes on the hope of that day whose promise is in night. The poem also grants a dawning answer:

like the salamander who is of night and of fire, Douve in herself will – perhaps? – resolve night. And as with the salamander whose face "was illuminated by those old trees for dying", with secretive Douve who need not be better known, her "face will catch fire". If there is no need for "lamps", strangers to the night, artificial recourse – perhaps in night itself the day will come at last, without abandoning the former?

> *Oh our force and our glory, will you*
> *Pierce the wall of the dead?*

It seems that *Hier Régnant Désert* is yet an answer to this last question of *Douve*.


The poem will soon release its lessons: "What did you want to raise on this table / If not the double fire of our death?", instruct as to the "state" of the follower: "Then I grew old. Outside, truth of speaking / And truth of wind ceased their struggle", to confide at last the price of that agreement (of night, of wind, with parlance, light): an almost painful appeasement of the once intransigent ambition to know. Does the agreement allow though for the unveiling of truth? Is knowledge achieved? For the moment, a double quality is imposed in *Hier Régnant Désert*, which emerges from intention itself, and in sum, from "departure".

This collection is more "abstract" – taking up some of what *Douve* had repudiated. Here the "law" takes form: each sketch of a conclusion implies a beginning of law. One share is granted to autobiography: it is no longer through Douve's bellowing and suffering force that the poet questions, but in the skin of memories, the humble gathering of efforts that enabled *Douve*, the places where

Douve did appear. The book thus recreates the sites of an adolescence. There, poetry is of the quotidian, a more exhaustive place is granted to the "lamp" of which it is said that it trembles "like a wounded bird charged with death".

This materiality is nonetheless no longer that of *Douve*, it refers to a precise reality. The poetics loses something of its perfection (in density), it gains in clarity of intention (in humanity). The collection seems both more immobile and more bruised, it suffers perhaps from presenting itself as the story of a quest, not as the quest itself and its fruit, offered in an indissociable pulp.

But the most precious asset resides here in a sort of open perspective. After the dense and nocturnal exploration of what figures truth, another of its dimensions, its becoming.

> *But the rains of night on the promised land*
> *Awakened the ardor that you call time.*

Here I see the beginnings of wisdom. And this is very much what dawn brings: a patience, a resolve to seek further in the day (say it, almost a diurnal program).

> *...........Will the ship of lamps*
> *Enter the harbor it had requested,*
> *Here on these tables the flame become ash*
> *Will it climb elsewhere in another clarity?*
> *Dawn, rise, take the shadowless face,*
> *Give color gradually to time recommenced.*

The poet will meditate on the always threatened perpetuity of truth, after having tried to startle its nature. He installs himself in this clear and humble "here"; perhaps will he divulge to us its "speakable desires": rendering to parlance, after the night of shards and silence, the simple dignity of its office.

What appears most fragile in this book, less dense, necessarily possesses the quality of the works of dawn: to be in a light that perceives itself before even having appeared. On the poet's road, *Hier Régnant Désert* offers no more conclusion than does *Douve*. We never attain to truth: but all poetry is accomplished through that quest.

There are thus amazements which do not leave you stupefied or stupid at the edge of some fabulous obscurity, destitute before a futile spark: which do not strike your eyes with blindness but, on the contrary, sharpen lucidity as if *over the top* of the gaze and beyond it. Thus the moment of dawn, so profitable for poets, where it seems that the being will wager himself in the fragile game of light. It is night, yesterday, memory burdened with its shadows, but tyrannically instructive, and it is already, total and unnoticed, and in stubborn pursuit of us, a Midi which is a present. Together poetic moment and place, the dawn reconciles these two "natures", which poetry continually brings together: the time that signifies us and the country that comprises us. There, it is not possible to distract savor from its duration, nor the heart from its history. Revelation is extended, but it does not temper the spark of its apparition; time constitutes itself there, but it does not begin, nor is it fixed: it *continues* for us, for our concern or our science, even when yesterday (by this night) it had left us.

Yves Bonnefoy's night sparkled in Douve. The night explored by Jacques Charpier is childhood, exalted, despoiled. It is the Time of the Dead (the Occupation), of caressed liberty; it is adolescence caught in a very concrete struggle.

> *Summer of pure kisses on the mouths of the dead!*
> *I can see them again, sniffed out by Lions and Shadows*
> *Your children, whom this wine of justice will intoxicate . . .*

The obstinacy in the past is reinforced in this presence. The dead – not an abstract death to be sculpted at leisure – come to speak again, at daybreak.

> *Oh virgin night that they made on my face!*
> *O wilted thorn of their names in stone!*

And not only the friend, the comrade, the brother, but mourned is the landscape: that winter has torn asunder. With the light of day the debate between the nocturnal and becoming begins. For to be an eternity of the instant, a fugitive palpitation of what lasts, twice does dawn anoint the poet: dramatic dialogue of he who struggles yesterday and of he who opts for the sun; revelation of the accidents of day, of the landscape's harvests, where a future that must be earned is divined. Struggling in his past, man rejects the solicitations of his diurnal double. Despite the recurred landscape, he answers invitations with a stubborn raising of death, now (and only now) known as sovereign mistress of his being.

> *Like a stalk shining in the mists of Scamander,*
> *From your lips apparent, a bit of dawn fled:*
> *Was it a game of old midnight? The heart of a bird beneath*
> *   the snow?*

> *It was of yesterday but a morsel, a wound*
> *Of the salt of memory forever harassed,*
> *A funereal bee resting on my lip . . .*

Pathetic and simple, and uncertain, this choir of responses. Constellated with several of the most beautiful images of contemporary poetry, yet without the imagery leading to troubled (and reassuring) delight.

> *Fire of ancient nights, oh my Empire!*
> *One thousand daggers make me one thousand smiles . . .*

(But the landscape was already victorious in being: such is the testimony of one of the poet's earlier works: *Mythologie du vent*. There the poetry inscribes the quest for unity in that same motion of time, which it will be necessary to lose – so that in the end its power may be measured, and for there to be no *end* to any of man's endeavors. Time begins with the "solitary initial of a love", and the questions draw from the nostalgic apostrophe of the first poem (of the first consciousness). But each answer is pressed against its outline, and love is enclosed in the earth that assists it:

> *In this country where there were henceforth too many days,*
> *I walked for a long time, sleeping only in those places where*
> *the ancient grasses had kept the initial of her body. And when*
> *she calls me, the clarity of her voice finding me in the solitary*
> *orchard, these are but almond trees of sorrow whose fruits she*
> *ripens.*

What grants this poetry its charm, what comprises its emotion, is that such a grave project – the meditation of time – was made sensible *by* a slow revolution of relations between a being and his country. And when, vanquished, the horror of the past surrenders to the knowledge of the past; when the gods, who had "covered [the poet's] brow with glacial myrtle", are the only ones who "languish after man"; when at last his real work begins, that of the *Séjour en terre humaine*, an earth having "escaped questions", with its weight of matter and of beauty; – only then does he cry out: "My face no longer has the past for a mirror", he consents: "I married the native land to an inaccessible time", and sings the pure poem of light.

This victory over yesterday (offering to yesterday) engenders its reward, which is knowledge of time as force and drive. Unfastening from time, the poet attains duration, which is like consciousness. He will soon want to return to the History that authorizes, when the dull rumor of the past was being obstructive. Already he ensures

> That from the stalk of wheat, harvested in silence, he made
> his blazon,
> And finds reasons in the beautiful mystery of duration.

Here it is important for the poet, in order to maintain this past in the "mad justice" of the sun, to learn to deliver it from its phantasms. The memory that does not rise to becoming becomes arid, projectless, an empty body "teetering on *its* buskins of dead wood".

> Like a beast that is led to covering
> You drag across the sky a funereal rose,
> O female darkness intermingled with me . . .

> O, I recognize you, Chimera! An infirm sun toward your
> spring is drawn,
> Misunderstood Power, sovereign Childhood,
> Like a splendid knife at the heart of our days!

Here then is the curvature of the earth, the patient work, man's hope and his humility; "Tomorrow is there, pushing its barge onto the beach . . ." Day grows in keeping with the calm beauty of its order, it invites night to the sun's feast. Debonair, sly, ferocious, this present sun is nonetheless our lot. The "old councillor" doesn't loosen his clutch. It is a failure to seek only the shadow of that which was our shadow and our night! Man betrays the night when, at the breach of Dawn, he still consoles himself or endlessly distracts himself from that past. To stiffen in his earth: "time purifying what does not abdicate".

And parlance spreads out into a very simple song, in which the quotidian has its part:

> *It's justice, to my liking, that of the past royalty comes to close*
> *Just as this snow does melt . . .*

But this past from which the poets extract themselves, this night that they leave, these dawns, this sun, this Place? Fragile – so transparent? Burdened so little by those concrete shudders, the quick of the world, *the deaths-of-others*, the black echoes? This past, mine? – Interred, mixed with unnamed earth, where consciousness drifts. And errance, precisely? Exile, more weighted by *residence*, exile of self and of one's land? My night, first night: when no one knew – do we know today, do we? – how troubling would be the weight of night to carry. This sun, pressured with temptations. This Place, so inexpert at carrying mass and granting cover, that drifts. Yet by honor and joy of current, it drifts to name the voices of the other on the shores of elsewhere. The naive dream of unity, so oft promoted, so distant then from its true and suffering becoming. The banal truths from which the arduous body must be forged. In every dawn that knot of rays, which communicates. Any sun is good, any past fertile; any voice competes.

One was quiet, another was reduced. The inability to write strikes everywhere. Obligation for the Occident of a language of tongues: the purification, by which one *followed the thread of the world*, is ruptured. Obligation to communicate, to say that one communicates, to not be a victim of speaking. The constitutive gaze is extinguished, each must constitute himself for the world. The alliance of the dream and action – was this not the noble underside of the desire for power? The One of Being has perished. For the Occident, obligation (consequently, and contrary) of a language before many languages. To be oneself in expression and no longer in expression for all. But the weight of consciousness is irreparable, such, today, is the restrictive advantage of *those who know*: they cannot forego a will to communicate which, for the best of their elders, was first a will to serve. The elders speak of action, the youngest of communication. The language of the elders is limpid and fragile, that of the youngest complex and brief. Then the will to communicate gains on the communicated itself. (The will to serve often masked action and the service to be rendered.) Thus to the generosity of action, the lucidity of the word wants to answer: fruitful duality prevailed.

This movement, did I not watch it "rush forth", at the very moment at which I was leaving Europe, *through* those whom I could not address at leisure – for they always gesture to me: from

Henri Pichette to Maurice Roche, my contemporaries in the space of away, the flexion of "serving" to "communicating"? The word, to itself ever sharper, ever more restive, more heavy, less spritely. Duality. Pichette who sang the universal world in his occupations and in his blood; and Jean Paris, one of the first in whom I encountered the exalted vision of inside-outside; Jean Laude, for whom this very heavy sand measured his gait; Pierre Oster, he encloses himself in days as in leaves of words; Jean Grosjean, I see the bronze humus with the joist of his farm, and from here I can leaf through his calm winter; Roger Giroux, the oldest and the youngest of the poets, whose temptation is silence and the torment of speaking it; and then Maurice Roche, who tattoos this pricelessness to relation: the horror of the word, the tracked word, the trembling snare for himself caught in words.

Yes. I see that movement of split parlance which, little by little, crouches, catches (I see it) –

Still, I hear the beating of another history, in the corner of the blacksmith's fire, the slow voice of Thomas Mofolo,
And, turning onto my flank, at the point at which that sea and that ocean are confluent
(At the pure injunction of commuting, where rupture was nonetheless never more surly),
As though from a spring here the beating of Nicholas Guillén's *éïas* surface
They walk on three legs for what they are dancing isn't so simple (here now, night),
The acacias grew on the morne at the foot of which the dogs once barked,
Here the cane fields end, the trace between logwoods disappears,

In this place the break between histories was marked, the return, in this place

The fugitive left the primordial night, entered the woods of becoming

(It's Wilfredo Lam's wake: jungle that is history and knowledge,

The density of being in stumps and roots known flesh of the unpenetrated.)

We are on our way, let's take the soil into our hands,

Cry out the odor of ancient bones.


The maroons hold an assembly in the clearing, which we pollard

(And those whom I have but named – they are more than one knowledge: one trail–

So near in time rejoined,

Lead to this stone, this feast.)

## Dreamed land, real country

Before midnight, the dogs gathered. They drifted within the limits of the alley. Solitary, united. Their occupation: to bark, interminable, seemingly joyful. Starved and ferocious. The cry was grouping their being! This is what is known as the Congress of dogs. That thunder enlarged the space of night, and in the distance became mixed with it like the heavy suspense of a trampled crowd, or perhaps the untethered expiration of a man's cry.

The latter beyond his renunciation in the neighboring renunciation. His earth is hailed with the spittle of another.

Teach depth. But depth is not of mystery; for us, it is in keeping with continuity. To follow the trace of red earth, from the heights all the way to the sea. Tomorrow, to discover the open.

We are clandestine. Hidden even from our own eyes.

In the memory I hold, this sky was not so covered in clouds. The sun stands to gain.

The earth at last, trembling. Balanced on the Pointe du Diamant to the West, the Caravelle to the East, it seeks every which way its due North. It leans: to measure the angle.

At Fonds-Massacre, is it necessary to mine the charnel house of the Maroons? At Salines, before the complicitous sea, you are excluded from your joy by so many arrogant comers. I am speaking to you of a future country.

Description of an island, fully removed from the world. Rocks in chaos or crouching. Grain of the sea, scorched winds! Unto the secret fracture that each man suffers, and of which – outside of his unremembered dreams – he never follows the trace but with the *fingers of words*.

Teach, that is: learn with.

To experience the landscape passionately. To disengage it from the indistinct, mine it, ignite it among us. To know what it signifies in us. To carry this clear knowledge to the earth.

If the solution seems difficult, perhaps even impractical, don't go crying out of the blue that it is false. Don't make use of the real to justify your lack. Realize instead your dreams in order to earn your reality.

Exalt the heat, fortify yourself by it. Your thought will be searing. We must despise air conditioners.

But the flash disperses. Crouches in continuity. Let's retie the ropes, mine some more. Become earthen and heavy.

Vomit each day of this common vomit.

Oh want, is it not time for you to defer to the black soil so many pettinesses that await only your cutlass? If you lack sky in order to dare live, go deeper, leave the spark of words, rummage through root. Then, as in so many childhoods of your design, you will speak of action.

Rumblings, these days: it seems that some discovered that this country must be decolonized. (That history does not march to the same beat for us.) (That we do not make our history to the very beat of the world.)

They called a hurricane what was a cyclone (thus they smother a share of their responsibility: a hurricane needn't be announced, and it is not so terrible). The rigors of our climate are not continuously excessive; but when violence is unleashed, it breaks. Happily, it does not last: nature is in the image of men, and the hurricane is of one night. But this accumulation of red mud, enormous stripped trunks, mad putridities knotted to the steel sheets of disemboweled cabins, the pestilence, or those derisory mattresses full of dry and irremediable viscosity, and more than anything, the slow resignation of the disaster victims: it is clear to me that our country covers itself with its true face, that the dull leprosy that gnaws at us, suddenly lifted by the waters, appears. It is always the destitute people whom the mud uproots. After these floods, there is no water left to soak the rags nor to give men drink. It doesn't rain (derision) and the dry plague besieges. It took four days for the authorities to think that it might be possible to feed the pumps with sea water (the inexhaustible sea that encircles and enjoins us), to clean up some of these ravages.

But it is impossible to use the sea.

We went – it is customary – to the Observatory of Morne-Rouge. Behind us the tough Pelée. Before us, the steep Pitons du Barbet to sculpt their dense vegetation. We could see, from each side of the narrowing cane, the sea to the West, the whitening ocean to the East. Beauty! that in this space of confinement, so many diversities are allied. The gigantic call of spaces is not to be regretted here.

Another time we climbed to the same post at nightfall. A layer of fog topped the world; we would have taken it for the cold of winter. But we couldn't lose ourselves: we were but simulating fear.

Just as the red earth to the black earth was mixed: one watches from the heights, the other is watched by malemort

Just as every word every spoken thing from before thickened, then, squared off, found its place in the speaking of days (you always speak the same word)

Just as the Caribbean Atlantic, which, whether twisted rock or sand spells out the same fate for

The quaking of the world where the new Water is born.


Just as at dawn the islands will carry you, old man: when beneath the stump the day's hook will have bored into the head and proclaimed the beast.


Just like the voice that hereabout gasps:
"Honor mocking serpent
for so long three Macabous keep watch
for our decomposed blood dried humus

*All has not been explored . . ."*


*Les Salines*
*December 1967.*

§ The texts that comprise the schematically "critical" aspect of this work were written for the most part between 1953 and 1961. They were the object of partial publications, principally in the journal, *Les Lettres nouvelles* and by the publisher, *Galerie du Dragon*. The pages devoted to Alejo Carpentier appeared in the journal, *Critique*.

§ All texts quoted by Glissant, including Hegel, as well as Faulkner, are translated from the French for this work. Since, in reading Poetic Intention one is reading Glissant reading, the greater concern is that line of relation, rather than an attested—or original—version.

§ Nathanaël is indebted to Anne Malena for her indispensable and meticulous labour and counsel through the work on countless drafts of the translation; and to Julian T. Brolaski, Jennifer Scappettone, Peter O'Leary and Christine Stewart for punctual dialogue regarding certain terms and formulations; Andrew Blackley for his keen eye. The last decisions regarding the text are the translator's sole responsibility; its awkwardnesses and turns.

To Stephen Motika, this very possibility, et à Édouard Glissant, pour m'avoir confié l'ombre de ses mots. N.

NIGHTBOAT BOOKS, a nonprofit organization, seeks to develop audiences for writers whose work resists convention and transcends boundaries. We publish books rich with poignancy, intelligence, and risk. Please visit our website, www.nightboat.org, to learn more about us and how you can support our future publications.

The following individuals have supported the publication of this book. We thank them for their generosity and commitment to the mission of Nightboat Books:

Sarah Heller
Elizabeth Motika
Benjamin Taylor

In addition, this book has been made possible, in part, by a grant from the New York State Council on the Arts Literature Program.

State of the Arts

NYSCA